CCCC Convention
Companion Publication

CCCC Convention Companion Publication
2024 Edition

Edited by

TIMOTHY OLEKSIAK
University of Massachusetts Boston

JAMILA M. KAREEM
University of Central Florida

AMY J. LUECK
Santa Clara University

LIGIA A. MIHUT
Barry University

National Council of Teachers of English
1 E. Main St., Suite #260, Champaign, IL 61820
www.ncte.org

Staff Editor: Kurt Austin
Interior Design: Jenny Jensen Greenleaf
Cover Design: Geno Church
Cover Artist: Remelisa Culitan

ISBN 978-0-8141-0227-5 (paperback); ISBN 978-0-8141-0228-2 (EPUB);
ISBN 978-0-8141-0230-5 (PDF)

©2024 by the Conference on College Composition and Communication of the National Council of Teachers of English.

All rights reserved. No part of this publication may be reproduced or transmitted in any form or by any means, electronic or mechanical, including photocopy, or any information storage and retrieval system, without permission from the copyright holder. Printed in the United States of America.

It is the policy of NCTE in its journals and other publications to provide a forum for the open discussion of ideas concerning the content and the teaching of English and the language arts. Publicity accorded to any particular point of view does not imply endorsement by the Executive Committee, the Board of Directors, or the membership at large, except in announcements of policy, where such endorsement is clearly specified.

NCTE provides equal employment opportunity (EEO) to all staff members and applicants for employment without regard to race, color, religion, sex, national origin, age, physical, mental or perceived handicap/disability, sexual orientation including gender identity or expression, ancestry, genetic information, marital status, military status, unfavorable discharge from military service, pregnancy, citizenship status, personal appearance, matriculation or political affiliation, or any other protected status under applicable federal, state, and local laws.

Every effort has been made to provide current URLs and email addresses, but because of the rapidly changing nature of the web, some sites and addresses may no longer be accessible.

Library of Congress Control Number: A catalog record of this book has been requested.

Contents

Foreword vii

1 *Abundance of Performance: Scarcity of Work in PTC Capstone Courses* 1
Kate Fedewa and Casey McArdle

2 *An Abundance of Awful: Using Weak Examples to Combat the Deficit Model* 11
Jennifer Gray and Stephanie Conner

3 *Quiet Rooms in Higher Education: At the Intersection of Scarcity and Abundance* 21
Melissa Guadrón, Addison Koneval, and Margaret Price

4 *Connecting Empathy with Research Trends in a Rhetoric and Composition Scholarly Publication* 29
Colleen Hart

5 *Writing the Story of Labor-Based Grading at an Urban Research University* 37
Adrienne Jankens

6 *Rhetorics of Refusal in Black Queer Femme Bravado Hip-Hop Music* 45
Christina Jordan

7 *Digital Multimodal Composition (DMC) Engagement in English Language Classrooms: A Pakistani Perspective* 52
Adeel Khalid and Fauzia Janjua

8 *Writing beyond Campus: Reflecting Critically on Abundant, Local Communal Knowledge* 62
Noah Patterson, Jacqueline Borchert, and Nathan McBurnett

CONTENTS

9 Ethos *in the Age of AI*................................. 70
    Pegeen Reichert Powell

10 *Reclaiming Latinx Rhetorics: Teaching Archival Research Writing to Spotlight Abundance in Students' Funds of Knowledge and Rhetorical Inheritances* 75
    Loretta Victoria Ramirez

11 *An Abundance of Voices: Examining Diverse and International Students' Assumptions about Writing to Cultivate Richer and More Inclusive Writing Classrooms* .. 82
    Yasmin Rioux

12 *Journal Writing in Abundance in First-Year Composition* .. 92
    Kylie Skeel

13 *A View from the ALPs: Teaching-Track Faculty and the Digital Pedagogical Mentorship of Graduate Student Instructors in the Active-Learning Pods Model* 99
    Gabrielle Stecher

14 *Black Community Colleges: A History and Appraisal* 106
    Howard Tinberg

15 *Decoloninzing Assessment to Reveal Abundance: Crafting Threshold Concepts and Mapping Learning Journeys* 117
    Jennifer Trainor, John Holland, Tara Lockhart, and Robert Kohls

Foreword: Historic Moment/What Is This?

This inaugural companion publication represents a significant landmark as CCCC celebrates 75 years of abundant work in composition, rhetoric, and literacy. Historical revisions are an opportune moment to define who we were and redefine who we are and what we do as an organization. As we reflect on what has been, is, and is yet to be, there is more than just celebration. This is not a triumphal narrative. As an organization, we have had racist, monolingual, and nationalist histories to confront as well as intentional and unintentional exclusions to acknowledge and rectify. We must not forget the outwardly prejudicial histories of CCCC, in which demographics who now enjoy full membership were relegated to partial, second-class participation. Whether segregating the presence and scholarship of its Black American members at mid-20th-century conferences (Mendenhall), upholding ableist and inaccessible policies and practices (Brueggemann et al.; Brewer et al.), denying two-year colleges a seat at the table, or disregarding queer contributions to the discipline, we must remember where we have been and what we have done to know who we are today.

In her 2024 Call for Proposals for the Convention with a theme of "Writing Abundance," Jennifer Sano-Franchini captures this insight by showing the growth of our organization not just in numbers but in range and depth. Sano-Franchini marshals abundant work of our members who have taught and conducted research in areas covering "African American, American Indian, Asian/Asian American, Latinx, Jewish, Islamic, Appalachian, queer/trans/LGBTQ+, disability, global, and feminist rhetoric, writing, and literacy studies; critical race theory (CRT) and antiracist approaches in rhetoric and writing studies; cultural rhetorics;

FOREWORD

environmental rhetoric and writing; digital, multimodal, and sonic rhetoric and composition; writing and rhetorics of code; community engagement; multilingual writing; writing centers; technical communication; and online writing instruction." We affirm with confidence that this *is* abundant work while also recognizing historical and ongoing efforts of many marginalized identities and their persistence in the fight for legitimation, participation, and full acceptance into this organization.

In an effort to further increase access and opportunity for all CCCC members to participate in the Annual Convention and enjoy the professional rewards associated with presentation and publication in CCCC venues, CCCC leadership took steps to create the CCCC *Convention Companion Publication*. The first of its kind for CCCC, the *Companion* is imagined as a space for those members whose proposals were accepted for presentation at the 2024 Annual Convention but who were unable to attend. These are contributions that enrich the intellectual work of the in-person Convention that would have otherwise been excluded. The *Companion* opens new avenues of circulation to make these contributions available to all members. The works in this volume represent the beginning of a response to the realities of multiple access and engagement needs of our members. It accounts for what our profession and CCCC must continue to grapple with: access and full participation in the knowledge exchange and professional development enjoyed by our most privileged members for our most marginalized members.

During the fall 2023 semester, a call for submissions was circulated among CCCC members. This call included an intention to submit. The lead editorial team—Jamila M. Kareem, Amy J. Lueck, Ligia A. Mihut, and Timothy Oleksiak—distributed submissions to our review team. The review team—Antonio Byrd, Kimberly Wieser-Weryackwe, Romeo García, and Zhaozhe Wang—offered reviewer feedback so that each submission received two sets of reviewer comments. Reviewers attended to the "Anti-Racist Scholarly Reviewing Practices: A Heuristic for Editors, Reviewers, and Authors" (2021) as a guiding metric for their reviews and highlighted areas where authors might strengthen their contributions. The lead editors then checked that the revisions were made and even offered, when necessary, our own feedback. The reviewers and editorial team offered light touches in line with acceptable review for conference proceedings rather than the kinds of engagements we'd have with manuscripts submitted to peer-reviewed journals. We wanted to maintain the energy of works-in-progress that is typical in a conference setting.

The submissions gathered in this conference companion represent a broad range of interests in our discipline. They are not polished articles, and should not be read as such. Instead, they are—as all good conference papers should be—provocations. Our hope is that this collection is similarly generative to readers, who might recognize even more abundance and opportunity at the intersection of these inquiries. As conference papers, these submissions are a promissory note for future research contributions from these authors, igniting curiosity and reflection among readers, and perhaps even spurring future collaborations.

The works in this collection reflect some of the less abundant voices of our community in many ways. We believe that these contributors can be productively read as interrupting the voices that have been overly abundant at our conferences. Such abundance comes most often in the forms of access to an abundance of funding for travel, an abundance of knowledge systems, an abundance of support. In addition to showing what we have in abundance, we must recognize and address what we need more of. We see this publication as a useful step in this direction.

Abundance of Use for Conference Space

Respecting the abundant points of view of our membership, this *Companion* intends to trouble the boundaries around what "conferencing" looks like and does, highlighting the abundance of uses to which such a convening might be put and the range of forms it might take. We all know there is already space within a convention to do multiple kinds of work—formal and informal, personal and professional, embodied and relational and theoretical and provisional. We come to the conference to get away and disconnect and to connect. We come to listen and to hear and to reconsider. We come to exchange and play.

Some of our members cannot join in that experience because of the specific conditions of their experience. This might include diminishing resources or health concerns, it might be due to family needs or other caregiving responsibilities, it might reflect the nature of their employment responsibilities, or any number of other reasons. This volume honors these choices via an extension of what a conference paper can do or be other than what is given in fifteen minutes of live speaking. Further, though, this *Companion* asserts that those conditions are not only barriers or deficits. They are part of the human experience of being a scholar alive and working in the world today. Their specificity and diversity enriches our disciplinary perspectives, providing texture and range to the insights we can make about language work. And these real human experiences need not prevent participation in the production and circulation of knowledge. This *Companion* acknowledges those difficult human choices that all scholars have to make in their careers, and provides a venue to mobilize them as potential intellectual resources.

In doing so, this *Companion* further expands what is possible, disrupting the normal convention time flows, extending them for the benefit of its members. It expands the boundaries of the exchange of knowledge, opening up space for yet another kind of work that might be considered part of our convening. It supports and extends the circulation of ideas that a conference is designed to encourage. Such new genres and modes of delivery intentionally exceed the boundaries of the conference space, redefining this work for the future.

Hope for the *Companion*'s Current Use and Future Possibilities

For all it does, this *Companion* still leaves many voices out. We would like to see this volume as a beginning, gesturing toward the need to expand further. In the future, perhaps this volume can transform into a Companion Blog, utilizing the affordances of online and digital writing practices that our field understands so well. The editors of this volume have similarly discussed the possibility of looping in the work of CCCC Documentarians to this project, pairing these projects in their kindred vision of an expanded array of roles for our membership to engage with the discipline, both on and off site. We have envisioned other interventions that are more inclusive and expansive: multilingual, multimodal, cross-genre, transnational, spanning appointment types and labor conditions. We invite you to be part of the imagining of this next horizon, imagining new genres and shapes of dialogue that can emerge from this.

In all of these ways, we hope that the *Companion*, in its present and future forms, productively challenges what convening looks like. The present barrier to engagement is simply acceptance of your CCCC proposal. As such, we hope you know and feel you are welcomed here. For our part on the Executive Committee and as part of the membership of CCCC, we commit to seeking more avenues to make that invitation meaningful.

For now, we hope you will use these visions as a guide to orient yourself toward the present contributions. Reach out to the authors here—provide feedback, cite them, and share resources to enrich their work like you would if you were in that conference room space together. Though the in-person experience is not replicable in the *Companion*, these are some of the gestures that readers might make to try to close that gap, and to open new avenues of abundance for the future.

Acknowledgments

Kristen Ritchie supported every person involved in this new effort. Both teams and contributors had questions, and Kristen's speedy and accurate responses made this process much smoother as a result. We want to thank Antonio Byrd, Romeo García, Zhaozhe Wang, and Kimberly Wieser-Weryackwe for their expertise and desire to support contributors with their careful and supportive feedback. We also thank CCCC leadership and the Executive Committee for moving forward with this new feature of CCCC. We hope that the ideas within are read, cited, and that the *Companion Publication* becomes a regular feature of the conference.

—Timothy Oleksiak, Jamila M. Kareem,
Amy J. Lueck, and Ligia A. Mihut

Works Cited

Brewer, Elizabeth, et al. "Creating a Culture of Access in Composition Studies." *Composition Studies*, vol. 42, no. 2, 2014, pp. 151–54.

Brueggemann, Brenda Jo, et al. "Becoming Visible: Lessons in Disability." *College Composition and Communication*, vol. 52, no. 3, 2001, pp. 368–98.

Mendenhall, Annie S. *Desegregation State: College Writing Programs after the Civil Rights Movement*. Utah State UP, 2022.

CHAPTER ONE

Abundance of Performance: Scarcity of Work in PTC Capstone Courses

KATE FEDEWA
Michigan State University

CASEY MCARDLE
Michigan State University

Introduction

In Carmen Kynard's 2020 article "'All I Need Is One Mic': A Black Feminist Community Meditation on the Work, the Job, and the Hustle (& Why So Many of Yall Confuse This Stuff)," she notes, "The conflation of the job and the work, however, is only possible for those groups sanctioned within the terms of a default white norm and privilege. It is easy to see the job as your work when the people and the culture around you are YOU" (19). As white program directors who teach PTC capstone courses at a PWI university, we struggle to distinguish between the job, the work, and the hustle and to help our students to do the same. And yet if we are to support young people—especially young people of color—in doing their important work, we must name these distinctions and recognize that the hustle is "a screen for white assimilation and really obscures the racial biopolitics of the processes" of career advancement in the academy and in industry (Kynard 18).

This article will discuss the evolution of two capstone courses as the result of our increased attention to Kynard's tripartite framework. We will describe the processes that helped us to recognize that our courses discussed the work but assessed—and thus prioritized—the job and especially the hustle. We describe how Kynard's article helped us begin to connect these gaps of abundance and scarcity so that we, and our students, could nuance discussions of professionalization, career readiness, and work. We also share revisions we have made to our courses so that our assignments and assessments align with learning outcomes that emphasize naming and addressing injustice, connecting with mentors and community, and acting through the core values that inform our work.

Our Process

In fall of 2022, we began to examine the capstone courses of our undergraduate programs (Professional and Public Writing, which is housed within our department, and Experience Architecture, which is housed at the college level, but administered in our department). We teach these courses and wanted to understand the relationship between the course content and our newly revised learning outcomes, which emphasized antiracist pedagogy. Our key frameworks for this examination were drawn from Kynard's "'All I Need Is One Mic'" and Walton, Moore, and Jones's 2019 book *Technical Communication after the Social Justice Turn*. Walton, Moore, and Jones provide their 4Rs as a heuristic for addressing systemic injustices:

1. Recognizing injustices, systems of oppression, and our own complicities in them,
2. Revealing these injustices, systemic oppressions, and complicities to others as a call-to-action and (organization/social/political) change,
3. Rejecting injustices, systemic oppressions, and opportunities to perpetuate them,
4. Replacing unjust and oppressive practices with intersectional, coalition-led practices. (133)

In bringing these frameworks to our own learning experience design, we discussed ways to enact Walton, Moore, and Jones's 4Rs as we planned our courses and ways to enact the 4Rs within our classroom communities.

Before the new semester began, we used the 4Rs to engage in an iterative design process that is grounded in continuous delivery (Beck et al.; Borgman and McArdle). We gathered old syllabi and assignments from both courses and then compared the content/skills students were developing with the content/skills assessed. We were mindful of Kynard's discussion: the tension in our outcomes and assignments between the hustle, the job, and the work revealed our courses' complicity in perpetuating an unjust system that rewards the hustle. Table 1 demonstrates how we framed these discussions.

As we began to recognize the injustices in our capstone courses, we revealed them, first to each other and then to the chair of the department and other faculty. With their support, we began the work of rejecting and replacing, again relying on Kynard's discussion. We repeatedly asked ourselves where our assignments, class discussions, and readings were emphasizing the hustle. At times this was obvious; for example, we recognized that previous iterations of an industry research assignment asked students to find salary information, specific positions and their

TABLE 1. Our application of Walton, Moore, and Jones's 4R framework via Kynard.

4Rs Step	During Course Planning	With Students
Recognize	Analyze learning outcomes and assignments using the work/job/hustle framework.	Discuss course learning outcomes and goals behind class assignments. Discuss "professional" as a problematic term. Review data around DEI in career search processes and in industry.
Reveal	Share results with other faculty, advisors, department chair.	Hold conversations with students around the tension between work, job, and hustle.
Reject	Identify and reject deliverables/assignments that emphasize hustle.	Build rubrics for assignments together to decide what should be assessed/given point value and what shouldn't.
Replace	Revise/replace hustle-heavy assignments with activities meant to help students consider their work.	Create space in the course schedule for student-directed discussions of work. Emphasize values-based reflection on all course activities.

workload, and entry-level opportunities but did not require students to consider power structures, workplace environments, or conversations around justice in their chosen industries. Other injustices were more subtle; only in our third or fourth review of our courses did we consider the ways in which the points students earned within the course valued hustle-related performances like resume-writing and mock interviews over deeper engagement with ideas of work or even an understanding of potential jobs. As the table above suggests, our course preparation required substantial revision and replacement at multiple points within our materials.

As we will discuss below, after using the 4Rs in our course preparation, we brought it to classroom discussions as well. We revealed systemic injustices (in industry [Wallet 2023; Oduwaiye 2020], in career searches [Haywood 2018; Hull et al. 2019], and in our own university systems and classes [Ahmed 2012; Boggs et al. 2019; Hull et al., 2019]) to students in our capstone courses as part of our classroom discussion. We hoped that each new moment of revealing would serve as a reminder of our own (and our program's) accountability and as an invitation for our students to think deeply about the work, job, and hustle as they prepared to graduate.

Identifying the Job, Work, and Hustle

Kynard notes that "the hustle" is in reference to "the ability to understand and navigate the arbitrary neoliberalist structures of the job market" (18). As administrators and educators, we struggle with the tension inherent in helping students engage with meaningful work while also securing positions to pay off student loans. We had long provided assignments that helped students with the hustle (e.g., resumes, cover letters, portfolios, interview skills, networking skills, and other performative content meant to help students get "the job"), but we recognized we needed to do better in helping our students do the work.

For example, in XA 466, the Experience Architecture capstone, a significant amount of time is spent on an XA Capstone Folder. Students engage in and reflect on experiences outside of the classroom to earn points (e.g., 10 points for attending an XA Club meeting run by students, 30 points for presenting at a conference, etc.) toward a required total. While intended to help students learn about their field and connect with mentors beyond the classroom, asking students to do these reflections and have these experiences to get a number of points has framed the assignment as the hustle. We must also acknowledge that nudging students via the Capstone into "professional" spaces can be harmful if the spaces and individuals they connect with are not supportive of marginalized groups or have practices that are against our program's values. Other assignments also prioritize the hustle: spending class time and grading elements of performances of professionalism, like resumes, cover letters, portfolio presentations, and so on. In our 4Rs process, we rejected the heavy emphasis in XA 466 on professionalization and professional documents as their own goal.

The 4R process here has been iterative; we continue to recognize more of our own complicity in perpetuating injustice within our classrooms. We created a Venn diagram of our course activities (see Figure 1) as a way to better visualize which assignments held which emphasis, all the while realizing that our framing of each assignment would also shape students' learning.

In reflecting on our courses, we noticed several activities that overlapped with work, job, and hustle; specifically, those that focused on reflection, the construction of a professional portfolio, various class discussions, and working with students to create rubrics for class assignments. For example, portfolios are part of the hustle as they are required to obtain jobs in our field, their creation relates to specific jobs because it requires students to learn/practice position-specific skills and genres, and the reflection underpinning portfolios is part of the work because students can identify and reflect on their values and the ways they are already participating in antiracist and justice activities. Other overlaps we found were networking and job fairs that we believe to be connected to both the job and the hustle, while community engagement and connecting with alumni were more between the job and the work. We also placed the analysis of job postings between the work and the hustle because students might examine a job description to see if it fits with their values and the work they want to do, and in doing so, utilize some hustle to get employed. Using Kynard's framework gave us a better understanding of these

FIGURE 1. *Diagram of the overlaps in our course activities between the work, the job, and the hustle.*

assignments and how our own course design was impeding our program goals. As we identified these overlaps, it became more apparent that our courses must help students tease out nuances between work, job, and hustle so that they could participate in any activity/module with the awareness of their own engagement.

We then situated our assignment revisions around making students aware of the distinctions and overlaps between the hustle, the job, and the work. For example, both classes, WRA 455 and XA 466, revised a research module on exploring career paths within industry into a module on understanding industries as systems and careers within them. Rather than just interview professionals and explore job titles for one module, students were required to explore DEI issues being discussed in the field and industry conversations and then to explain how they are related to potential spaces they wished to enter after graduation. This allowed us to recognize and reveal the hustle, and also to equip students with the skills to actually do the work many came to our program willing and hoping to do. Each class utilized a document template for students to use and collect data from their research to inform their approaches when entering the job market. Below is an excerpt from XA 466 with distinct directions for the students as well as a link to a template for them to use:

> **Requirements**
> To complete this module you need to compose a variety of texts—here is a <u>link to a template</u> that you will use.
> - Find sectors associated with XA you are interested in
>   - UX Research
>   - UX Design
>   - Web development
>   - Deceptive patterns
>   - etc.
> - Find trade journals or trade publications where these sectors are being explored
>   - *UXPA*
>   - *Journal of User Experience*
>   - etc.
> - Explore DEI issues that these sectors are having
>   - What are the hiring practices of these sectors?
>   - How are these sectors handling accessibility?
>   - What kinds of support do they provide for marginalized groups?
>   - etc.
> - Interview **3 people** in these sectors—questions should be informed by your work above.
>   - Include interview notes.
>   - Include interview reflection.

Previous iterations of these requirements asked students to focus their research on specific positions, salaries, and skill sets for those positions. After viewing this research project through the 4Rs and Kynard's work, we felt revising this module was essential so that students might rhetorically analyze their future industries as complex systems and determine where safe and unsafe spaces may exist for them and their work.

Conclusion

Our courses encourage students to identify and live their values, to believe they can build coalitions with peers to critique unjust systems and build toward better spaces; our courses also teach students the "professional" genres, moves, and strategies to participate in those same systems. In our revisions and our replacing, we noticed students responding to this ongoing tension in different ways. Some did deeper dives on workplace DEI with articles and research that summarized the issues in those work spaces—even revising their interview questions to ask alumni specifically about DEI (this was not the case pre-revision in both courses). Other students did surface-level reflection and engagement with work-related assignments. Some reported feeling overwhelmed at the weight of such large questions; others simply said that they were seniors, they were tired, and MSU had been through a lot over the past few years, especially in spring of 2023.

At the end of the fall 2023 semester, students from both classes presented their senior portfolios to alumni, faculty, and their peers. Through faculty observations, we noticed two distinct differences between the students in the programs:

1. P2W students were generally focused on introducing themselves and their philosophies. For example, students were saying: "Hi, my name is ___. I am an empathetic editor who listens to clients."

2. XA students were generally more focused on showcasing their work. For example, students quickly pulled up case studies on their portfolios and walked attendees through their process, iterations, and deliverables.

Although we did not see these differences as drawbacks, it was enlightening to observe how students in each program framed their work, job, and hustle. P2W students shifted from emphasizing hustle to narrating the importance of leadership, listening, and collaboration. XA students used deliverables to demonstrate their ability to take on various roles within the career force and prioritize inclusive systems. The students' transition was evident, but it fell short of embodying Kynard's ideals. Kynard describes the work as supporting students of color and addressing systemic inequity; while our students mentioned antiracism and inclusivity as values, only a few students had fully articulated their "whys" and imagined what their work might look like in career, civic, and other spaces. Essentially, we made progress, but there is still more work ahead.

Our work then, is incomplete, and the data noted above reveals the same about our institutions and industry. Kynard's insight into how we can change these spaces, when combined with the work of Walton, Moore, and Jones, gives us hope that we can support students to undo systems that prioritize the hustle over the work.

Works Cited

Ahmed, Sara. *On Being Included: Racism and Diversity in Institutional Life*. Duke UP, 2012.

Beck, Kent, et al. "The Agile Manifesto." Agile Alliance, 2001, https://agilemanifesto.org/.

Boggs, Abigail, et al. "Abolitionist University Studies: An Invitation." Abolitionist University, 2019, https://abolition.university/invitation/.

Borgman, Jessie, and Casey McArdle. "Continuous Delivery: A PARS Online Course Development Cycle." *Computers and Composition*, vol. 66, 2022.

Haywood, Constance. "Headwraps and Hoops in TPC: Decolonizing Professionalism through Dress and Work Practices." Panel Presentation. Association of Teachers of Technical Writing, 2018, Kansas City, Kansas, USA.

Hull, Brittany, et al. "Dressed by Not Tryin' to Impress: Black Women Deconstructing 'Professional' Dress." *Journal of Multimodal Rhetorics*, vol. 3, no.1, 2019, http://journalofmultimodalrhetorics.com/3-2-hull-shelton-mckoy.

Kynard, Carmen. "'All I Need Is One Mic': A Black Feminist Community Meditation on the Work, the Job, and the Hustle (& Why So Many of Yall Confuse This Stuff)." *Community Literacy Journal*, vol. 14, no. 2, 2020, pp. 5–24.

Oduwaiye, Ann. "Black Women in UX: The World Was Not Designed for Us, but It Can Be Redesigned." 2020, https://www.linkedin.com/pulse/black-women-ux-world-designed-us-can-redesigned-ann-oduwaiye/.

Wallet, Ben. "Your UX team Isn't Diverse Enough, despite Your DEI Efforts." 2023, https://bootcamp.uxdesign.cc/your-ux-team-isnt-diverse-enough-despite-your-dei-efforts- 4342740d5d46.

Walton, Rebecca, et al. *Technical Communication After the Social Justice Turn: Building Coalitions for Action*. Routledge, 2019.

Chapter Two

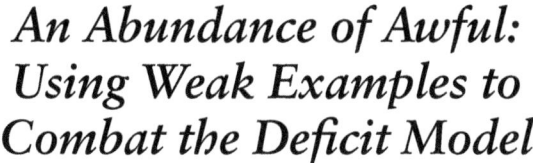

An Abundance of Awful: Using Weak Examples to Combat the Deficit Model

Jennifer Gray
College of Coastal Georgia

Stephanie Conner
College of Coastal Georgia

During assignment sequences, students are typically shown examples of ideal projects, often called mentor texts. Textbooks are full of strong student examples that highlight what a stellar response to the assignment would be, and many writing instructors utilize this activity. However, only using strong elements ignores two valuable lessons to be learned from critically analyzing awful examples. First, when students are able to explain the weaknesses within bad examples, they understand concepts on a deeper level and apply them to their own work. An abstract concept like citation conventions becomes concrete upon viewing, experiencing, and discussing lousy examples. Second, looking at weak examples shows students that writing does not appear in perfect form immediately. Work must be polished and revised; looking only at beautiful, strong examples makes this messy revision work hidden.

Using examples and discussion to show how students benefit from exploring weak real-world published documents and websites can help students critically pick apart the inherent issues related to the significant concepts of information literacy and user experience (Council of Writing Program Administrators and National Writing Project). By studying bad example sources, students can examine their processes and explore different options that can be used to improve written products. Students learn what to avoid and why, strengthening their own critical thinking about their work.

Mentor Texts

Modeling writing via a mentor text has long been an effective component of writing instruction. A mentor text is a sample piece of writing that serves as a guide for a writer, and writing instructors are encouraged to use class time and homework assignments to engage with models of what an assignment can be (Campbell and Latimer). These models could be professional published pieces, work from the instructor, and current or past student writing. The strategy of using mentor texts can improve students' writing process because the mentor texts provide a window into unfamiliar written products and genres. Students can dissect what is working in a mentor text and then apply that discovery to their own written products as they experiment with the assigned genres in their courses. The mentor text provides a direction, which can be especially helpful for inexperienced writers who may have a limited toolbox of strategies (Rose). However, mentor texts need to be used with caution, as there are some pitfalls to exclusively using strong mentor texts.

When students see only polished final versions, their expectations for their own writing can be unreasonable, as they do not see the mess and work involved in creating the final version; sometimes, they even feel they are not good writers, and they should be ashamed of their work (Whitney). They feel deficient. Students compare their in-process and unfinished early work to finished products; this comparison can make students feel like they do not belong, their language and voice are not valued, and/or they are not able to write well, much as Donald Murray described in his noteworthy piece on the importance of process. Many college assignments, such as an essay, are presented as an unchanging and fixed entity that follows a strict and rigid structure that must be mimicked in order to achieve success (Gannon). For students who struggle with writing confidence, this rule-following can be intimidating and overwhelming. It can lead to writing avoidance when students see the writing as directly connected to their own self-worth (Whitney). If the writing is not any good, then they must not be any good. Mentor texts show only the clean, properly formatted, and editorially sound versions of work, which can increase students' anxiety and their own writing discomfort.

One way to help with student anxiety is by using weak mentor texts to both bolster critical thinking and build writer confidence. A weak mentor text is a piece of writing that fits within the general guidelines of a project a student might be working on, but this sample writing is not stellar. There are inherent problems or omissions within the writing that are easily visible, and these lacking or lousy elements become the entry points into a discussion and critique about the sample writing. It is important to note that we are not trying to shame students or highlight actual weak student writing; instead, the weak writing comes from existing published pieces readily available online through a simple internet search. These weak sources exist in everyday life, and they illustrate the practical challenges of writing. They also illustrate that writing is not perfect, and students should not expect perfection from their own writings. The weak sources are selected based on course learning principles, such as elements of strong sources (author, date, experience) or adherence to suggested criteria (design elements discussed during class). The sources may be selected by the instructor or the students.

Our goal is to provide readers with some practical examples taken directly from our classes. Jennifer will begin by discussing a major assignment in her 1000-level writing course, and Stephanie will then discuss an assignment in her 3000-level Technical and Professional Communication course.

First-Year Writing Course: Jennifer

In my course, one major assignment focuses on the credibility of sources and their evaluation. I focus on improving students' abilities to evaluate and select sources to strengthen their writing. We begin with an activity focused on credibility with a commonly known concept, Lasik eye surgery. I use a source that was organically discovered using a Google search with "Lasik" as the only search term. This source was listed within the first few pages of the results, so the source represents an authentic result students might find. I describe my search process and where this source appeared within the list of results. I talk to students about their own searching process, what types of sources stand out to them in lists of results, and how many pages of results they seek. See Figure 2.1 for the homepage of the website (www.lasikathome.com), which provides an overview of the product.

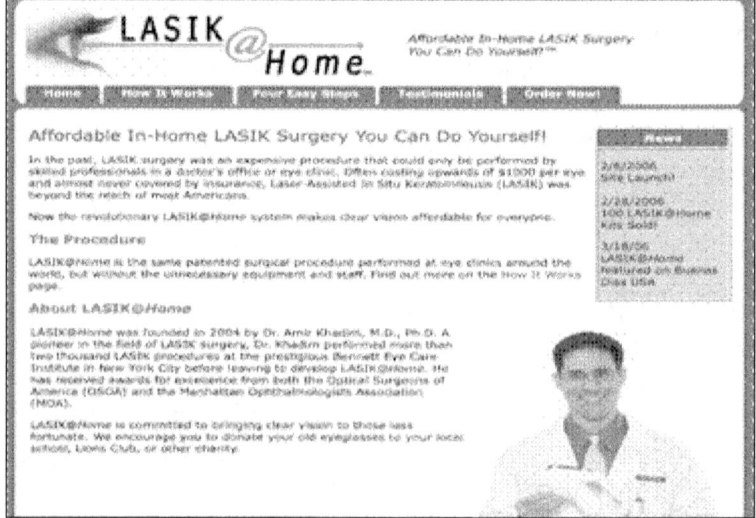

FIGURE 2.1. *Lasik @ Home homepage.*

While this source is not a legitimate source, it does appear in a list of results like a legitimate source would. Students look at the source collectively, and their reactions range from delight to suspicion to confusion. Many students automatically assume that the source is real, especially after we have the discussion about our searching processes. The existence of a fake product disrupts their comfort with believing the internet. They ask questions such as "Why is this source available?" We talk about the elements that feel real, such as the layout and the appearance of an expert with the ethos of degrees and titles. We highlight the importance of taking time to evaluate the sources we use in life.

An Abundance of Awful: Using Weak Examples to Combat the Deficit Model

We then move to the next section of the website, "How It Works," which includes a brief description of the device:

FIGURE 2.2. *"How It Works" page from Lasik @ Home website.*

We talk through the features on this page that highlight the process of the Lasik at home procedure and its contents. We discuss the safety message and ponder how the warning includes not looking at a laser, which seems to contradict what happens during a Lasik procedure. Students dwell on the name of the machine, "Scal-Pal," which sounds quite painful. Toward the top of the page, there is a point about where and how the materials are made, with a message about how this machine is "used by more clinics nationwide." Students ask what "more clinics" means in this case, and we have the opportunity to talk about how results or satisfaction data are shared in public documents. We usually conclude with a quick mention about the material with the asterisk, which indicates that the FDA has not evaluated these statements.

The bottom of this page leads us naturally into the next section, "Four Easy Steps" (see Figure 2.3), which teaches readers how to use the product.

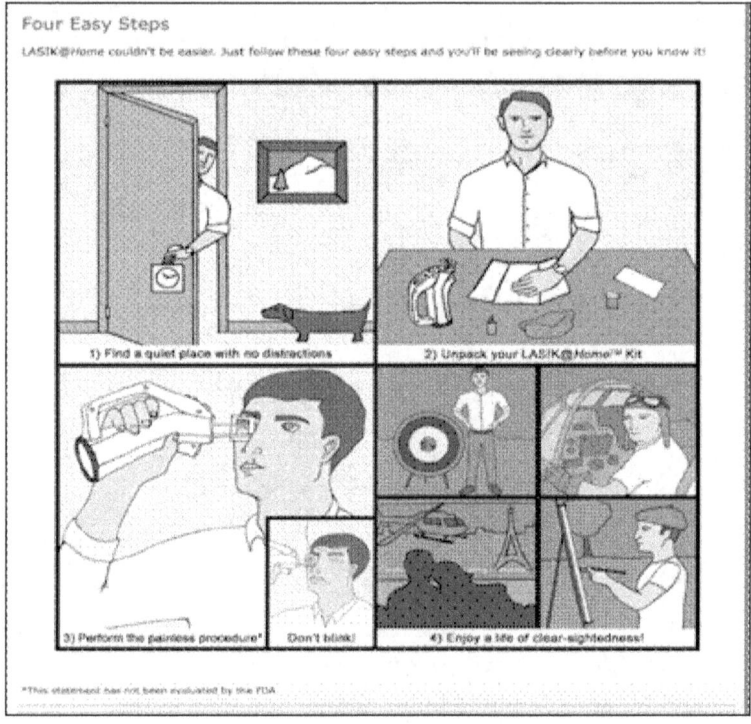

FIGURE 2.3. *"Four Easy Steps" page of Lasik @ Home website.*

This page generates laughter. Students remark that this page looks like a furniture assembly direction sheet, and they are stunned at the "Don't Blink" panel. We remark on how the informal tone and childish drawings decrease their confidence in the product. We talk about the repeated FDA asterisk statement, and they are confused about how this material is online and visible to any viewer. This point is a great time to talk about how just because something is online does not mean the material is accurate.

After reviewing the entire website, I ask students to do their own searches for Lasik and share the results. They bring up journal articles about Lasik studies or they find organizations or government documents focused on the procedure. Students share their findings either in class that same day or for homework the next day, and they gain a sense of confidence about their abilities to find strong sources. They have a clear understanding of why the quality of a source impacts their selection, and sharing their reflections and results publicly with the class provides even more examples of quality sources. The information comes from the students, not the professor, so students remember and integrate the findings into their learning. This activity results in a memorable, vocal, and hands-on experience for students that helps them think about the quality of sources they are using in their projects. This skill is something they can take with them into their future.

Technical and Professional Communication Course: Stephanie

Technical and Professional Communication is a course designed to introduce students to professional writing. Often, students who enroll in this course have a good understanding of written content but not as much of an awareness of the importance of design elements in constructing documents and other technical media. For example, the layout of a resume will either ensure the clarity and highlight necessary skills and qualifications, or it will obstruct readers from finding important information.

As a way to engage students with learning about and recognizing strong design elements, I first provide a knowledge base for them to work from. We discuss the CRAP strategies (Contrast, Repetition, Alignment, Proximity) developed by Robin Patricia Williams and look at different examples of each strategy. Then, I ask them to find an example of bad design already published online that does not follow the CRAP strategies, share it with the class, and apply the strategies we've discussed. In contrast to Jennifer finding a weak example and then using it in class, this course, at the 3000-level, asks students to find the weak source that does not adhere to the strategies discussed. The students become responsible for locating the weak source.

Unsurprisingly, students present each other with fantastic examples of problematic design like the website https://www.arngren.net/ (Figure 2.4), which is a collection of items for sale.

Figure 2.4. Page from *www.arngren.net* website.

While sharing the gnarly designs with each other is a fun way to engage with the material, the analysis of the designs is where the learning happens. Some of our observations include the lack of adherence to CRAP strategies and the inability to read the text or see the pictures as individual units. We have noted how the website's design complicates the buying process and how the random use of color and fonts is confusing for users. Much like Jennifer's source credibility assignment, this ability to recognize essential design techniques and presentation are skills that will translate into many professional situations.

Implications for Practice: A Sticky Memory

The key element to using weak mentor texts is what happens *after* students view the weak materials. In addition to commenting and identifying the weak elements, they then need to take time to re-vision the weak materials. They can do this by revising the material to strengthen the content. In Jennifer's assignment, students spend time finding strong sources that repair the problems they noted in the weak source. In Stephanie's class, students highlight the issues with the websites and discuss what could be done differently. The discussion and reflection helped them integrate and apply the points they discussed to their own future works. All of these re-visioning skills work to improve upcoming projects for students; in essence, the experience becomes a sticky memory that can be called upon for future writing occasions. Students can call back to the classwork re-visioning experience to improve their own writing projects and information literacy. And they do all of this knowing that this written work does not appear in perfect form. They see the weaknesses and see the active choices that need to be made to improve the strength of the project. This experience of re-visioning the work sticks with students and improves their confidence, as they have direct experience of taking an actual published work and thinking about how to re-vision that work to make it better.

So, what do we gain from looking at the worst? While strong mentor texts can provide students new to a particular type of genre foundational knowledge and confidence, focusing only on strong examples limits the active learning gnarly examples can generate. One reason is that bad examples are everywhere. They are easily accessible and connected to students' own life experiences. They also have the power of humor. In an online class, especially, creating strong assignments that generate delight can go a long way to creating camaraderie and cohesiveness. Having students find, examine, and reflect on bad examples reinforces abstract concepts we usually only talk about in class. Students can draw from real-world examples beyond the academic classroom and integrate those examples into the learning dialogue. As they reflect on the weaknesses and omissions, they are reflecting on strengths needed for each assignment as they learn about different genres and writing occasions.

Works Cited

Campbell, Kimberly Hill, and Kristi Latimer. *Beyond the Five-Paragraph Essay*. Stenhouse, 2012.

Council of Writing Program Administrators et al. *Framework for Success in Postsecondary Writing*, 2011, https://wpacouncil.org/aws/CWPA/asset_manager/get_file/350201?ver=7548. Accessed 12 January 2024.

Gannon, Kevin. *Radical Hope: A Teaching Manifesto*. West Virginia UP, 2020.

"Items for sale." www.arngren.net. Accessed 12 January 2024.

LASIK@Home. 2006, www.lasikathome.com. Accessed 12 January 2024.

Murray, Donald. "Teach Writing as a Process not Product." *The Leaflet*, vol. 71, no. 4, 1972, pp. 8–10.

Rose, Mike. "Rigid Rules, Inflexible Plans, and the Stifling of Language: A Cognitive Analysis of Writer's Block." *College Composition and Communication*, vol. 31, no. 4, 1980, pp. 389–401. https://doi.org/10.2307/356589.

Whitney, Anne Elrod. "Shame in the Writing Classroom." *English Journal*, vol. 107, no. 3, 2018, pp. 130–32. https://www.jstor.org/stable/26450183.

Williams, Robin. *The Non-Designer's Design Book*. 4th ed., Peachpit Press, 2014.

CHAPTER THREE

Quiet Rooms in Higher Education: At the Intersection of Scarcity and Abundance

MELISSA GUADRÓN
The Ohio State University

ADDISON KONEVAL
The Ohio State University

MARGARET PRICE
The Ohio State University

Introduction

In "The Importance of Keeping Quiet Rooms Quiet," Leslie R. Anglesey and Ellen Cecil-Lemkin document misuses of quiet rooms (QRs) at conferences, including talking aloud or holding meetings. Lack of access in QRs is not just a matter of individual action: as Anglesey and Cecil-Lemkin note, structural barriers may encourage misuse or even make a QR unusable. Anglesey and Cecil-Lemkin remark that "disabled scholars are frequently called upon to do the labor of creating accessible environments, in much the same way as marginalized groups have long been required to do the invisible labor of cultivating a space that is less hostile to their presence" (102). As three of the people who founded a permanent QR in our workplace, we're especially interested in the structural forces that may complicate or even foreclose users' experience of QRs.

From 2021 to 2023, we conducted an exploratory study to learn about the experiences of our QR users. Our primary finding is that *a QR is likely to house a collision of many different needs in* the face of almost uniformly inaccessible workplaces / educational spaces. QR "fails" documented in research are, therefore, not anomalies, nor are they small-scale problems with easy fixes. Given the larger contexts in which QRs are typically installed, they seem almost set up to fail—or at least to face significant challenges. The culture of scarcity in most schools and workplaces is intense enough that QRs almost inevitably become spaces of *access friction*, a concept we draw from Aimi Hamraie and Kelly Fritsch's "Crip Technoscience Manifesto," which defines "access-making" as "a site of political friction and contestation" (n.p.). Access is always a process, and that process is always entangled with political, historical, and social conflicts (see also Smilges, *Crip Negativity*).

According to research participants, our institution's QR is used for purposes including physical rest; work; escape or respite from work; privacy; de-stimulation; and impromptu private meetings. Drawing on our findings, we argue that attention to the uses of QRs in academia reveals crucial pressure points for precarious academic workers. These pressure points include scarcity of resources, including space; hierarchies in rank; users' minoritized or multiply minoritized positions; and lack of control over temporality. As such, continuing attention to the use of QRs can help academics create more just and accessible spaces for academic workers, not only in QRs but also beyond.

QR Overview + Methods

In 2019, the Graduate Association of Mental Health Action and Advocacy (GAMHAA) began a mission to create a permanent QR at Ohio State University. We three, as part of this organization (i.e., its graduate officers and faculty advisor), imagined the QR as a direct contrast to areas of campus that centered hyper-productivity and socialization. Our proposal envisioned the room as a low-stimulation, anti-work space specifically for graduate students and associated faculty (i.e., academic laborers without private offices).

Quiet Rooms in Higher Education

FIGURE 3.1. *Part of the GAMHAA QR in 2019.*

FIGURE 3.2. *An image of a "cubby spot" in the GAMHAA QR.*

With support for our proposal from all the necessary university administrators, GAMHAA partnered with Ohio State's English Department, the Disability Studies Program, and two local businesses (M+A Architects and Continental Office) to design, install, and furnish a permanent QR in the English Department's building. We repurposed a shared graduate student office and spent months working with our partners on drafting blueprints, cleaning and painting the former office, and securing funding for furniture. Meanwhile, GAMHAA opened multiple channels of communication with graduate students to solicit opinions on potential blueprints and items for the room. M+A Architects, along with providing blueprints, donated requested items such as a white noise machine, weighted blanket, and sunlamp. GAMHAA then worked closely with the English Department's communication team to design signage for the room outlining rules for accessing and using the space (see Figs. 3.3 and 3.4).

FIGURE 3.3. *Signage posted outside the QR's door with information on using and accessing the space.*

FIGURE 3.4. *Signage posted inside the QR with rules for using the space.*

Chief among these rules were prohibiting use of the room as a workspace or office. Instead, we encouraged users to take a nap on the couch, meditate, or curl up with a book. With the onset of COVID-19, work on the QR stalled. After petitioning the university to release our funding (due to an institutional freeze), the project was completed and the GAMHAA QR officially opened in November of 2020.

We hypothesized the GAMHAA QR would be used as a space to escape the pressures of working in the academy. A little over a year after the opening of the QR, we tested this hypothesis with an Institutional Review Board-approved study on user experiences. Our research questions investigated how users felt about the QR and how they occupied the space. Taking a grounded theory approach (Glaser and Strauss), we analyzed surveys from 14 QR users and interviews with 6 of those same users. During analysis, we examined what participants understood the QR to be about (in terms of major issues, themes, and questions) and how they developed their understanding of those issues, themes, and questions.

Results

We found significant access friction that challenged our initial assumptions about how individuals would use the space. While our data showed evidence of multiple expressions of access friction arising with the QR, for this article, we focus on "rest" (deliberately not working) versus "respite" (privacy for various activities, including work).

Rest: A Need Met for Disabled Participants

Especially among self-identified disabled QR users, the QR filled a need for rest—for intentionally not working. Graduate student Thelonius (this, along with all other participants' names, is a pseudonym) shared that he used the QR "to be alone," and take a break from work. To Thelonius, the QR, unlike his shared graduate office, was a space where he could leave work aside and do something like read for pleasure: "I really want these two areas of my life to be very, very separate, very clear line of demarcation between business and unwinding," he said. Furthermore, the QR also offered a much-needed social reprieve. Thelonius noted that he works better "in isolation," adding, "anytime I'm in my office alone, then it's always like, 'Alright. This is nice.'" In contrast, interacting with others he was unfamiliar with felt "weird" and prompted uncertainty about how much to engage in settings like the graduate student lounge. In contrast, the QR allowed for rest through non-work infused privacy not often available to graduate students.

Similarly, graduate student Daisy explained she used the QR to rest and de-stim. "[De-stimming] means to get myself back in my body, and also to release some of the tension that's built up inside of it. So [Daisy] in, tension out," she said. To de-stim, Daisy preferred to lie on the couch, napping or reading a book in the QR's low-stimulation environment, the latter aspect of the room being crucial because, as she told us, "I have the autistic, very sensitive hearing paired with the ADHD awful auditory processing." The privacy afforded by the QR, along with its intentional design, created a unique campus space for Daisy to rest in ways she couldn't elsewhere on campus.

Respite: An Access Friction

While "rest" was a common theme among disabled participants, we found that the QR fulfilled a related but distinct need for "respite" more generally among academic laborers lacking the private space, control over time, and resources that tenured academic laborers had. Here, while "rest" signaled reprieve from work, "respite" did not. Graduate students' need for respite was intertwined with wanting to reclaim control over their time and responding to the university's social culture of performance.

Participants who did not identify as disabled reported primarily using the QR as an alternative workspace. However, their reasons for working in the QR differed. MFA student Sam worked in the QR on days when she had a long break. She said that one term she "taught in the morning from like 11:10 till 12:30, and then I had class at 5:30. . . . So then I was like, OK, what do I do with like five hours?" On these days, she "would try to stick around campus" and "try to finish all the poems for workshop." While she attempted to work in communal spaces, like the library, her office, or the graduate lounge, she said it could be difficult to focus in such social spaces.

Two additional participants spoke to social dimensions of pressures and precarities unique to graduate students. On the one hand, Coral saw the QR as "a haven-like, shelter-like place for me amidst this pressure-some working environment." On the other, Nina stated that she preferred the QR as a *private* working space: "I just like it better than the library because I don't feel so like watched or like perceived," she said. These precarities result from insufficient private, individual workspaces.

Similarly, associated faculty member Ann expressed a desire for a private working space—but her need was grounded in having a space to conduct the interpersonal aspects of her job. As a full-time instructor who shares an office with four others, she remarked that her office is rarely quiet or private. This raises several challenges, like having insufficient space for student conferences or having private space to talk with students about sensitive topics, like bad grades and personal struggles. In the past, Ann would hold student conferences in the English Department's lactation room, but she "had colleagues who were nursing, and [...] didn't want to take the room from them." So, despite signage that discourages conversation in the QR, she confessed that if the room was empty, she'd "love to be able to take a student in there for a private conversation when they're like crying and telling me about, like, their grandma, who died." She felt these interactions were inappropriate to conduct in her shared office.

Discussion: The Quiet Room as a Nexus of Access Needs

In evaluating the uses of the QR for rest and respite, we found a disparity which provides a telling example of access friction. Self-identified disabled participants reported using the QR almost exclusively for rest, which aligned with our original vision for the space. In contrast, participants who did not identify as disabled used the QR as an alternative space for work. Although the latter group treated the QR as an extension of the workplace, these participants also relied on this space for privacy and quiet.

The competing uses of the QR reveals a variety of resource-related needs for academic laborers, including lack of privacy, lack of control of one's workspaces or schedules, lack of time or space, and/or an access need. These exigencies revealed pressing precarities related to both the nature of being a graduate student or associated faculty member *and* insufficient institutional accommodations for disabled users.

Our study demonstrates how a QR becomes a magnifying glass for the inequities of the institution. Particularly in academia, where space and time are used as mechanisms of privilege and oppression, a QR will emphasize how those privileges and oppressions operate. Our exploratory study shows that significant issues include distinguishing between "rest" and "respite." We urge other researchers and storytellers to take up our work and continue exploring the meanings, impacts, and insights of QRs—permanent and temporary, ad-hoc and planned well in advance. QRs are an important access measure in institutional spaces, but perhaps even more important is investigation of the negative space they carve out—that is, the "non-quiet" rhetorical situations from which we need respite.

Works Cited

Anglesey, Leslie. R., and Ellen Cecil-Lemkin. "The Importance of Keeping Conference Quiet Rooms Quiet." *College Composition and Communication*, vol. 72, no. 1, 2020, pp. 99–102.

Glaser, Barney, and Anselm Strauss. *The Discovery of Grounded Theory*. Routledge, 1967.

Hamraie, Aimi, and Kelly Fritsch. "Crip Technoscience Manifesto." *Catalyst: Feminism, Theory, Technoscience*, vol. 5, no. 1, 2019. DOI: https://doi.org/10.28968/cftt.v5i1.29607.

Smilges, J. Logan. *Crip Negativity*. U of Minnesota P, 2023.

CHAPTER FOUR

Connecting Empathy with Research Trends in a Rhetoric and Composition Scholarly Publication

COLLEEN HART
Wayne State University

Background

By creating scarcity in publishing, disciplinary journals maintain a hierarchy of "good" academic scholarship and a monopoly over who determines what scholarship is valuable or credible. Venues including academic websites and journals publish content reflecting the national pulse, often responding to national concerns (see Wallace and Zamudio-Suarez for data on trending topics in *The Chronicle of Higher Education* in 2023), yet a wealth of untapped or undervalued knowledge exists outside mainstream academic publishing. Publishing decisions are jointly made by reviewers and editors as a means to curate scholarship that aligns with a journal's scholarly aims, but these traditions can have negative impacts of upholding structural racism amongst others (Cagle et al.). Malea Powell reflects on the restrictive nature of publishing regarding diversity in the disciplinary journal *College Composition and Communication* (CCC), pointing out work to be done in these spaces. By exploring what topics are published in mainstream scholarly journals, we can identify missing topics in these disciplinary conversations and begin to address how to incorporate more scholarship about these marginalized topics in future publications. Therefore, in this paper I present quantitative research regarding subject key terms used by authors published in

CCC which offer an abundance of data—over 1,300 individual terms between 2001 and 2021. Subject key terms (SKT) are assigned by authors to identify the topics of their articles, and they are used by disciplinary journals and article databases to group articles based on topic and by researchers as a mode to find them. As the flagship journal of our discipline, I had high hopes for finding inclusive publication trends in *CCC* because in their call for papers, the editors invite "research and theories from a broad range of humanistic disciplines—English studies, linguistics, literacy studies, rhetoric, cultural studies, LGBT studies, gender studies, critical theory, education, technology studies, race studies, communication, philosophy of language, anthropology, sociology, and others" ("Write for CCC"). This encouragement of interdisciplinary scholarship and incorporation of many subfields should indicate a diverse range of research published here. Consequently, I explore how topics including empathy, feminism, and race are represented in this data and conclude that the gaps in publication on these topics indicate a need to actualize publishing on marginalized issues rather than express aspirations to do so.

I begin this research with an exploration into empathy and feminist studies, my area of study. Situating my research amongst divisive rhetoric stemming from events including 9/11, and more recently, the 2016 and 2020 presidential elections, empathy is increasingly relevant as a topic of conversation and research. Additionally, within rhetoric and composition studies (RCS), the habits of mind listed in the *Framework for Success in Postsecondary Writing,* such as understanding and care, express the values of our disciplinary community for the classroom; therefore, I expected that RCS would encourage these habits in other spaces. What at first seemed like guaranteed success in my trek through 20 years of *CCC* article publications soon became a slough for any scrap of data relating to empathy. Interest in feminist scholarly trends in RCS is not new; LaFrance et al. argue for the importance of "continu[ing] conversations about *what we most value as researchers and how that makes a difference to our discussion of research practices, knowledge construction, and conventions of publication*" (594, emphasis in original). Rather than considering research methods as they were performed by LaFrance et al., this paper explores the SKT data to do such work by tracing publication trends relating to feminist studies and other minoritized topics of research in RCS, and, ultimately, consider how these conversations might be better taken up in mainstream academic journals.

Methods

Rather than exploring subjects of article publications through content analysis, my approach to collecting data was to utilize the terms authors already use to describe their own research, i.e., SKT. In my collection of SKT, I utilized the scholarly database ProQuest's digital listing of CCC publications which were organized by publication date, including month and year, and listed chronologically from the print publication's page order. In my collection I did not include the table of contents, CCCC news pages, or announcements and calls. Additionally, articles without SKT listed were not included in the study. This is important to note because in many of the earlier years of the journal, articles frequently did not list SKT. "From the Editor" articles were included, as well as "CCCC Exemplar Award Acceptance Remarks" and "CCCC Chair's Address." When SKT were listed, articles dedicated to the memory of scholars who have passed and anonymously authored articles were also included in the data set.

I located the SKT through the abstract/details page listed in ProQuest for each article. SKT were hyperlinked under the section listed "subjects," and I copied and recorded these SKT in an Excel spreadsheet, organized by year of publication. To avoid missing articles, these terms were recorded chronologically based on publication order by month and author last name. I then created a second Excel page organized again by year and alphabetized by SKT to remove author names and identify repetitions of SKT. Between 2001 and 2021, 902 articles were included in this study and each year averaged 42.95 articles published.

Results

Data

Within the 21-year range of article publications, I found 1,346 unique terms used as SKT. Each seasonal publication in 2009 produced a significantly larger number of articles compared to preceding and subsequent years, which has a notable impact on the data collected and analyzed in this paper. During this search, I found *empathy* used as an SKT in two articles, once in 2008 and once in 2013. Because of empathy's infrequent use as an SKT, I did explore other SKT relating to empathy, including *mindfulness*, used once (2019), and *emotions*, used three times (2014, 2016, 2019). Because the SKT *empathy* and related terms did not garner results, I widened my search to a more generalized term, *feminism*. This search proved more fruitful because *feminism* appeared 30 times. Based on the trend line (the lighter line) in Figure 4.1, over the 21-year period, the term *feminism* is used twice as much at the end of the data set as at the beginning.

Diving back into the data, I explored trends relating to diversity. I searched for the use of terms *diversity* and *inclusion* as SKT which, surprisingly, were not used as SKT. Despite being broad terms, perhaps these terms did not accurately represent

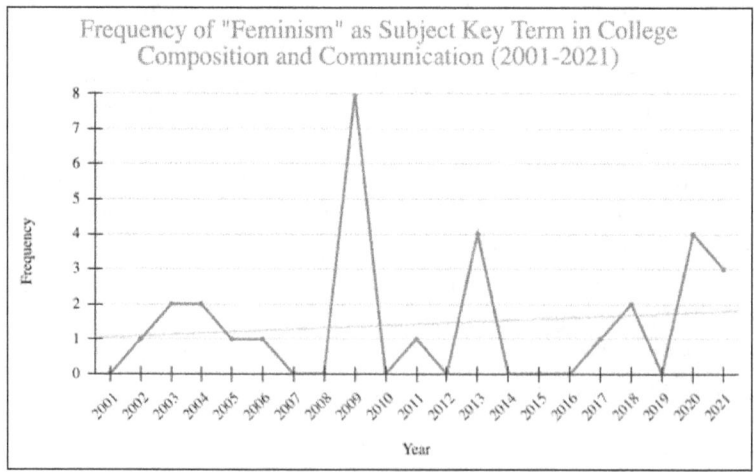

FIGURE 4.1. *Frequency of* Feminism *as Subject Key Term*

article content or methods. Then I explored SKT relating to race studies, disability studies, and LGBT studies. For length, I will focus on findings relating to race studies. Multiple SKT were included to track trends relating to race studies, including *race, racism, racial identity, racial discrimination, racial difference, racial justice, racial relations, racial violence,* and *critical race theory*. As can be seen in Figure 4.2, these terms are used infrequently, sometimes finding multiple-year trends but no major trends across the entire selection of years. Similar to Figure 4.1, there is a gap relating to race just as there is a gap relating to feminism during the early 2010s.

Implications

All of the data presented here shows major gaps in publication on the topics of empathy, feminism, and race. The two uses of empathy as an SKT between 2001 and 2021 publications of CCC indicates no article publication trend for this term. One word out of over one thousand SKT, used twice out of thousands of uses during 2001–2021, shows no statistical relationship. Here lies the conflict: while empathy was not used as an SKT, that is not to say that empathy is not expressed in the publications in other ways, but perhaps its representation is not understood as such. However, there is value to using this term, specifically, to describing research in RCS, and its absence points to a larger

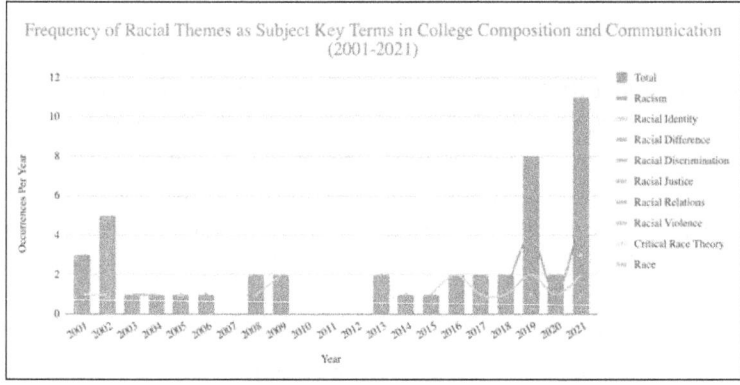

FIGURE 4.2. *Frequency of racial themes as subject key terms in* CCC.

disconnect between the assignment of SKT and how they are used by researchers to find articles. As such, the *absence* indicates that SKT may not correlate with values of the field or trends in scholarship. The data presented on feminist studies and race studies showcases similar gaps. *Feminism*'s inconsistent use as an SKT offers no clear trend and points to no relevance to major conversations in the field. On average, the use of *feminism* as an SKT is 1.43 times per year; considering that there are on average 42.95 articles published per year, the term *feminism* is not used often at approximately 3% of articles per year. SKT relating to race studies shows similar unclear trends, but perhaps indicates a trend of increasing publications relating to this area of research. The increase in the use of terms related to race as SKT only begins around 2019, so it is unclear if this is the beginning of a focus on this area of study; however, it is clear that prior to these most recent years of data included in my study, there were not major trends relating to research in this area as published by CCC.

Conclusion

In this paper, I surveyed all SKT from 2001 to 2021 published in *CCC* articles to discover publication trends about empathy, and, additionally, publications of feminist studies and race studies. The 902 articles surveyed here offer 1,346 research topics, and one imagines no rock unturned in the research published in *CCC*. But a lackluster showing of research on empathy indicates SKT offers potential to understanding more about how research functions in our discipline, what trends can be seen, and what topics are valued in prominent RCS journals. During her editorship at *CCC*, Malea Powell notes her approach to diversifying the journal through cultural rhetorics, starting with "revis[ing] the journal's mission to match that of the [conference] as an organization" as well as creating a reviewer "tag" system to better align manuscripts with more appropriate reviewers (210). While these are major steps toward this effort that may not be represented in the data set I have collected, there are still more actions to be taken regarding creating inclusive publication trends. A similar tagging system might be able to be adopted to allow an editor access to an author's varied positionalities, but a simpler solution might be, as Kelly Blewett and authors point to, soliciting manuscripts from diverse authorship rather than "depending on diversity to follow in the flows of existing channels" (286). Additionally, the *Anti-Racist Scholarly Reviewing Practices: A Heuristic for Editors, Reviewers, and Authors* created by Cagle et al. offers many actions to support diversity in scholarship that are impactful beyond their subdiscipline of professional and technical writing, including professional organizations offering mentoring to authors on how to frame their scholarship or creating a process for appeals when issues arise in the review of manuscripts.

While this research is a not a comprehensive review of all topics present in CCC scholarship, it does offer insight to where issues may exist in the publication of diverse and inclusive research. Additionally, it offers potential actions to be taken in the publication of scholarly research in order to expand publications in these areas.

Works Cited

Blewett, Kelly, et al. "Editing as Inclusion Activism." *College English*, vol. 81, no. 4, 2019, pp. 273–96.

Cagle, Lauren E., et al. *Anti-Racist Scholarly Reviewing Practices: A Heuristic for Editors, Reviewers, and Authors.* 2021. Retrieved from https://tinyurl.com/reviewheuristic.

Council of Writing Program Administrators et al. *Framework for Success in Postsecondary Writing.* Jan. 2011. http://wpacouncil.org/files/framework-for-success-postsecondary-writing.pdf.

Graban, Tarez Samra. "From Location(s) to Locatability: Mapping Feminist Recovery and Archival Activity through Metadata." *College English*, vol. 76, no. 2, 2013, pp. 171–93.

LaFrance, Michelle, et al. "Fingerprinting Feminist Methodologies/Methods: An Analysis of Empirical Research Trends in Four Composition Journals between 2007 and 2016." *College Composition and Communication*, vol. 72, no. 4, 2021, pp. 570–600.

Powell, Malea. "Making Space for Diverse Knowledges: Building Cultural Rhetorics Editorial Practices." *Behind the Curtain of Scholarly Publishing: Editors in Writing Studies,* edited by Greg Giberson et al., UP of Colorado, 2022. ProQuest Ebook Central, http://ebookcentral.proquest.com/lib/wayne/detail.action?docID=6970776.

Wallace, Claire, and Fernada Zamudio-Suarez. "2023: The Year in Higher Ed." *The Chronicle of Higher Education,* Dec. 20, 2023, https://www.chronicle.com/article/2023-the-year-in-higher-ed.

"Write for CCC." *College Composition and Communication.* NCTE. https://cccc.ncte.org/cccc/ccc/write, par. 1.

Chapter Five

Writing the Story of Labor-Based Grading at an Urban Research University

Adrienne Jankens
Wayne State University

Regional and national audiences are familiar with the story of Wayne State University's attention to graduation rates for Black students, with news outlets sharing the crucial statistic that in 2011, the graduation rate for Black students whose parents also attended college was only 9% (Huffman). In 2012, *Bridge Michigan*, a nonpartisan, online magazine, published a story by Ron French, "At Wayne State, easy to get in, difficult to get out," in which the author cited the university's "liberal admissions policy and tough academic standards" as part of the reason for dismal graduation rates for Black students. Though these rates have been improving, during the COVID-19 pandemic, nonproductive grade rates for minority students in general education composition courses rose sharply. The reality of this juxtaposition of student-success forces has driven our composition program to work persistently to improve curriculum, instruction, and general student support for first-year students, including the wide-integration of antiracist writing instruction practices. It is widely understood that success in our FYC course is a predictor of student graduation within six years (Pruchnic et al.). However, in local news outlets and even in university announcements and newsletters, the work of first-year general education instructors is left out of these stories.

In this paper, I describe the design of my assessment of the integration of labor-based grading in FYC, one of these instructional approaches, to understand teachers' experience of using this "antiracist" practice at an institution where over 50% of students self-identify in racial and ethnic categories other than white. Scholarship describing labor-based grading often examines the work of individual instructors or classrooms (Inoue; Gomes et al.; Santos; Mateo-Girona and Dean; Sims). Change work often seems most possible at the level of the individual classroom, where WPAs may allow instructors to employ their choice of well-founded yet unofficial projects or assessment schemes. However, writing programs require more than "passive agreement" with these antiracist approaches; they require the active implementation of curriculum, professional development, and administrative policies and processes that directly support antiracism (Branson and Sanchez 71). Without input from the range of instructors and students working through these initiatives, they will not be sustainable, and their actionability unsure (Allan et al.; Osorio et al.). The assessment I describe honors instructors' experiential evidence through the implementation of a reflective writing construct integrated as one vertex of a reflection-assessment-development triangle (Allan and Driscoll), immediately supports local teacher development and program assessment, and responds to scholarship urging the inclusion of the voices of marginalized and contingent instructors in the development of writing program initiatives (Allan et al.; Cole and Hassel).

The employment of labor-based grading in any given context requires attention to the specific conditions of that context. Recent critiques demonstrate the ways labor-based grading may reify inequities and continue to leave specific groups of students at a disadvantage (Kryger and Zimmerman; Carillo). In response to possibilities and tensions discussed in scholarship and practical discussions with teachers over several years, I have developed a model of labor-based grading that I think and hope both suits WSU students' learning and work lives and functions practically in the structures of face-to-face and online courses. I was invited to include my model in our program's new common syllabus for FYC. While there is not space to describe it in depth here, this version is technically simple and includes labor-based descriptions of assigned tasks, complete/incomplete assessments, and the opportunity for students to revise and resubmit. It is based on ten years of experimentation and revision in my own classroom; however, whether and how it works in other teachers' classrooms is something to know more about.

The pilot assessment I am conducting of the integration of this model is funded by a college-level social justice initiative grant and focuses on the following questions:

- What do instructors' written reflections on integrating labor-based grading practices into FYC convey about their experiences employing specific practices (e.g., complete/incomplete grading, student conferencing, student revision, rubric design, etc.)?

- What do instructors' written reflections on integrating labor-based grading practices into FYC convey about needed revisions to the existing documented process or instructor support materials?

- What are instructors' resource needs (training sessions, mentoring conversations, instructional materials, scholarly texts, etc.) for implementing this labor-based grading model in FYC?

To collect artifacts for assessment, I invited GTAs in my fall 2023 practicum to participate anonymously in twice-weekly reflective writing tasks adapted from Lindquist et al.'s Documentarian surveys. These tasks engaged GTAs in preflection, documentation, and reflection (Lindquist and Halbritter) on their integration of labor-based grading. At the beginning of each week, I asked participants to preflect on the following:

- What teaching tasks lie ahead of you today and this week?*
- How are you feeling about these tasks? Uncertain? Confident? Organized? Overwhelmed? Excited? Something else?*
- What will happen in your ENG 1020 class today (or later this week)?
- How do you expect your ENG 1020 class to go today (or later this week)?
- What labor-based grading practices will you be working on this week in your ENG 1020 class (e.g., working with written feedback, reviewing a rubric, reflecting on writing process and

labor, conferencing about projects, making decisions about the components of a project, adjusting your feedback practices, etc.)?*
- What about these labor-based grading practices feels challenging in your work with your ENG 1020 class?*
- What about these labor-based grading practices feels positive?*
- What questions do you need answered (by your students, by your peers, by Adrienne, by other Composition Program faculty, by others) to help this week's teaching work go as you plan or hope?

Then, as they finished their teaching that week, I asked them to reflect on the following questions, echoing the ideas in the beginning-of-the-week survey:

- What teaching tasks did you work through this week?
- How do you feel about these tasks now that the week is wrapping up?
- What happened in your ENG 1020 class this week?*
- Who or what shaped your teaching plans, changes to your teaching plans, your response(s) to students, and/or your classroom activity this week? How?
- What labor-based grading practices did you work on with your ENG 1020 students this week (e.g., working with written feedback, reviewing a rubric, reflecting on writing process and labor, conferencing about projects, making decisions about the components of a project, adjusting your feedback practices, etc.)?*
- How do you feel about how you (and students) engaged these practices this week?*
- What resources would have better supported your work with labor-based grading this week?*

While I wanted to offer flexibility in the labor participants would choose to put into completing the survey, the required, asterisked questions would provide us with a sense of the rhythm of the course, participants' feelings about labor-based grading, and needed resources.

In winter 2024, I will seek participation from these GTAs in a one-day, paid assessment activity. The session will integrate layered reflection, collaborative coding, and discussion to identify themes based on the experiential evidence present in survey responses (Teeters and Potvin). Brief memos outlining these themes will inform the design of a teaching workshop and needed instructional support materials for the program LMS. While I await this session, I can provide a preview of our story through the results of brief surveys sent at the beginning and end of the semester.

In the introduction survey, I first asked participants to "List one, two, or three words that describe how you're feeling about teaching ENG 1020 this semester." All eight teachers invited to participate responded:

- Overwhelmed, excited, confident
- Nervous, overwhelmed, hopeful
- Anxious, excited
- Supported, annoyed
- Excited, comfortable, open
- Nervous, self-conscious
- Nervous and like I've been thrown into the deep-end
- Confident, "mostly" prepared

Nervous is chosen as a descriptor by three participants, and I see a mix of words with positive and negative connotations describing participants' feelings about teaching this class.

Then I asked participants to "List one, two, or three words that describe how you're feeling about using labor-based grading this semester." They responded:

- Intrigued, positive
- Intrigued, happy
- Worried, overwhelmed
- Positive, insightful

- Interested
- Optimistic, relieved
- Apprehensive yet positive
- Intrigued, excited

Intrigued and *positive* stand out, each used three times. Overall, the words participants chose are positive, with the exception of one participants' response that they were *worried* and *overwhelmed* by using labor-based grading.

A conclusion survey mirrored the introduction survey. Five teachers participated. About teaching ENG 1020, they shared feelings that tended toward the positive and evidence the complex emotions of teaching:

- Now that it's done, I am so relieved. During the semester, it was stressful to say the least.
- Frustrated, overwhelmed, motivated
- Rewarding, enjoyable
- Rewarded, challenged, exhausted
- Confident

About labor-based grading, these teachers shared more mixed feelings:

- Still unconvinced
- Ambivalent
- Still skeptical
- Inspired, motivated, overloaded
- Mostly good

Participants' feelings about teaching ENG 1020 and their feelings about labor-based grading, as a whole, seem to have flipped across the semester, moving from mixed feelings about teaching 1020 to generally more confident or motivated, and from invested in or curious about labor-based grading to perhaps more incredulous.

For me, this reinforces the idea that contract grading must be designed according to the conditions of learning in an individual classroom—the features of a labor-based grading scheme, specifically, need to reflect the expectations and agreements of the larger classroom ecology to feel appropriate and manageable. But what that specifically means for this cohort of teachers and for our program at Wayne State is to be discovered through our collaborative assessment.

Works Cited

Allan, Elizabeth G., and Dana Lynn Driscoll. "The Three-Fold Benefit of Reflective Writing: Improving Program Assessment, Student Learning, and Faculty Professional Development." *Assessing Writing,* vol. 21, 2014, pp. 37–55.

Allan, Elizabeth G., et al. "The Source of Our Ethos: Using Evidence-Based Practices to Affect a Program-Wide Shift from 'I Think' to 'We Know.'" *Composition Forum,* vol. 32, 2015. https://compositionforum.com/issue/32/oakland.php.

Branson, Tyler S., and James Chase Sanchez. "Programmatic Approaches to Antiracist Writing Program Policy." *WPA: Writing Program Administration,* vol. 44, no. 3, 2021, pp. 71–76.

Carillo, Ellen C. *The Hidden Inequities in Labor-Based Contract Grading.* Utah State UP, 2021.

Cole, Kirsti, and Holly Hassel. "Introduction: Transformations in a Changing Landscape." *Transformations: Change Work Across Writing Programs, Pedagogies, and Practices,* edited by Holly Hassel and Kirsti Cole. Utah State UP, 2021, pp. 3–16.

French, Ron. "At Wayne State, easy to get in, difficult to get out." *Bridge Michigan,* 28 Feb. 2012. https://www.bridgemi.com/talent-education/wayne-state-easy-get-difficult-get-out.

Gomes, Mathew, et al. "Enabling Meaningful Labor: Narratives of Participation in a Grading Contract." *Journal of Writing Assessment,* vol. 13, no. 2, 2020. https://escholarship.org/uc/item/1p60j218.

Huffman, Bryce. "Wayne State University Aims to Increase Graduation Rate." *Morning Edition.* NPR, 14 May 2019. https://www.npr.org/2019/05/14/723135026/wayne-state-university-aims-to-increase-graduation-rate.

Inoue, Asao B. *Labor-Based Grading Contracts*. WAC Clearinghouse, 2019.

Kryger, Kathleen, and Griffin X. Zimmeran. "Neurodivergence and Intersectionality in Labor-Based Grading Contracts." *Journal of Writing Assessment*, vol. 13, no. 2, 2020, pp. 1–12.

Lindquist, Julie, et al. *Recollections from an Uncommon Time: 4C20 Documentarian Tales*. CCCC/NCTE, 2023.

Lindquist, Julie, and Bump Halbritter. "Documenting and Discovering Learning: Reimagining the Work of the Literacy Narrative." *College Composition and Communication*, vol. 70, no. 3, 2019, pp. 413–45.

Mateo-Girona, M. Theresa, and Christopher Dean. "Digital Writing and Labor-Based Grading: An Equitable and Inclusive Approach to Undergraduate Writing Instruction." *Perspectiva Educacional*, vol. 62, no. 2, 2023. http://dx.doi.org/10.4151/07189729.

Osorio, Ruth, et al. "Braiding Stories, Taking Action: A Narrative of Graduate Worker-Led Change Work." *Transformations: Change Work Across Writing Programs, Pedagogies, and Practices*, edited by Holly Hassel and Kirsti Cole, Utah State UP, 2021, pp. 19–36.

Pruchnic, Jeff, et al. "Slouching Toward Sustainability: Mixed Methods in the Direct Assessment of Student Writing." *The Journal of Writing Assessment*, vol. 11, no. 1, 2018. https://escholarship.org/uc/item/9z65k7wj.

Santos, Marc C. "How I Implemented Asao B. Inoue's Labor-Based Grading and Other Antiracist Assessment Strategies." *CEA Critic*, vol. 84, no. 2, 2022, pp. 160–79.

Sims, Mikenna Leigh. "Shifting Perceptions of Socially Just Writing Assessment: Labor-Based Contract Grading and Multilingual Writing Instruction." *Assessing Writing*, vol. 57, 2023. https://doi.org/10.1016/j.asw.2023.100731.

Teeters, Leah Peña, and Ashley Potvin. "Collaborative Qualitative Coding." UC Boulder. Accessed 14 January 2024. https://www.colorado.edu/crowninstitute/sites/default/files/attached-files/evaluate_and_iterate_collaborative_qualitative_coding_v4.pdf.

CHAPTER SIX

Rhetorics of Refusal in Black Queer Femme Bravado Hip-Hop Music

CHRISTINA JORDAN
The University of Texas at San Antonio

Geneva Smitherman argues that hip hop has always "been outside the mainstream of white American values. Implicit in their outsider status is a rejection of the narrowness of mainstream white America with its rigidity, provincialism, and racism" (23). Hip hop was born from Black oppression in the United States, and using it as a catalyst for change within the current, "whitewashed" educational structure is vital for social justice and equity in the classroom because it "engages in conversations of, with, and about Black bodies in various manifestations of rhetorical resistance as intellectual and intersectional identities" (McGee 53). In other words, providing curriculum that focuses on Black culture and history can lead to equity in classrooms. Hip-hop music is not only versatile, but it is also relevant to what many students are listening to on a daily basis, so embracing it as inspiration to encourage a cultural understanding of marginalized people is essential. Exploring the theme of writing abundance as a methodology by assessing how hip-hop artist Lil Nas X rearticulates heteronormative and patriarchal ideals in American society, by refusing and resisting preexisting standards of power dynamics for marginalized groups in an effort to display nonnormative "standards" of being, is necessary for the inclusion of all people. The popularity of hip-hop culture has already set a precedent for linguistic ideas to emerge within society, creating a "new language that reflects a dynamic blend of traditional and innovative linguistic patterns," otherwise known as African American English (AAE) (Smitherman 11). Allowing AAE to be present in the classroom creates a space for Black youth to feel empowered and heard because it validates their language practices. April Baker-Bell states that it is imperative for Black students to use a "language that explicitly names and richly captures the types of linguistic oppression that is uniquely experienced and endured by Black Language speakers" ("We Been Knowin" 7). She knows the complexities of how Black language functions and does not function within educational institutions, and she argues how schools should adopt "Antiracist Black Language Pedagogy," which involves three key factors: it must "center Blackness, confront white linguistic and cultural hegemony, and contest anti-Blackness" (Baker-Bell, "Dismantling" 8). Applying hip-hop music as a focal point in the classroom hits at all three points. Along those same lines, in *Digital Griots* Adam Banks reveals the importance of DJs and hip-hop artists to "provide the figure through whom African American rhetoric can be reimagined in a new century" (Banks 3). Their music can be revolutionary because it expresses the social, political, and mental struggles people of color face; "technology and education collide with and exacerbate long-standing inequalities that we must rethink old problems" (Banks 5). Including hip-hop music in the classroom, especially from diverse artists, allows for students and teachers alike to understand the complexities of being a person of color and pushes for "other" narratives (such as those of the LGBTQ community) to endure within an educational structure that is lacking in heterogeneity.

The ways in which Lil Nas X reappropriates Black culture using what I term Black Queer Femme Bravado through his inclusion of genderfluidity and open homosexuality within hip-hop culture breaks the barriers between the heteronormative, misogynist, and sexist genre hip-hop once was into a new generation of inclusive music that is revolutionary. In short, Black Queer Femme Bravado is an ideology rooted in Blackness that explains how artists embrace speech, fashion, and demeanor typically taken on by hypermasculine men to reverse heteronormative ideals speaking to who and what can be masculine. It subverts the notion of binary existences, but instead calls to fluidity within the stereotypical feminine and masculine constructs in American culture. Lil Nas X uses Black Queer Femme Bravado in his music videos as a form of refusal of the heteronormative stereotypes in American culture. When he embraces this phenomenon as a performance by depicting queer circumstances within his music videos, he defies the status quo, allows space for all voices to be heard, and provides opportunities for people to reconstruct what love looks like and how it functions within the nonbinary. For those reasons, incorporating Black Queer Femme Bravado in curriculum through Lil Nas X's musical influence and aiming for students to utilize and write about its core components positively reinforce the importance of inclusivity in classrooms. In her work "Diversity and Writing: Dialogue within a Modern University," Jacqueline Jones Royster argues, "The key to success may actually be in getting the empowered to recognize how each human being in relation to other human beings is something, if not always, 'other' for any number of reasons" (17). Royster's work brings about a new way of incorporating inclusion into the classroom—by addressing how each person functions in relation to others, privilege-wise. Providing hip-hop music, specifically Lil Nas X, as a source of conversation and identification for students will begin to tear down the views of seeing some only as "other."

    Lil Nas X's visual representation of queer love in his music videos is unlike any other artist's attempt to reveal same-sex love. Jaymi Leah Grullon[1] affirms, "Lil Nas X represents a queerness that is politically and formally against heterosexual forms—a refusal to participate in the institution of Straight Time[2]" (15). Lil Nas X is brave and goes beyond the bounds of people's comfort zones, allowing himself and his dancers to not only be naked, but wear make-up, dress femininely, dance provocatively, and show physical attraction to the same sex through their use of touching, groping, kissing, and caressing, which are all aspects of Black Queer Femme Bravado. Lil Nas X's music video "That's What I Want" begins with him being shot out of the sky onto a football field. He is injured, so he gets carted to the locker room. At first, the audience does not know why he is upset, other than him not being able to play, but moments later, another player arrives who he apparently was waiting for. They begin making out and though it is not shown, they go further to have sexual intercourse. Aside from Lil Nas X's obvious openness with gay sex, his incorporation of depicting a sport that is typically seen as masculine in such a way that shows members of the team in bright pink uniforms and behaving in ways that are more feminine is transformational. He consistently adopts aspects of Black Queer Femme Bravado with his use of images geared toward heteronormativity that strips them of those classifications and reverses the interpretation to include and showcase homosexuality and the nonbinary.

In the next scene of the music video, he is on a date with that same man from before—they are camping in the woods and dressed in a typical "cowboy" persona. Seconds into the scene, it shows the two men in their tent, partaking in another sexual encounter, elevating Lil Nas X's consistent use of flooding people's screens with images that may make people uncomfortable. Award-winning writer, culture critic, and English professor Eric Darnell Pritchard believes, "Black queerness helps us to recalibrate our view so that we can see what we thought we knew differently and look beyond what already exists" (241). So, for Lil Nas X in a multitude of queer circumstances, he wants people to become desensitized to these images so they can accept the various ways people love, as well as reconstruct what love looks like and how it functions within the nonbinary.

In the second-to-last scene between these two gentlemen, Lil Nas X approaches his boyfriend's house with flowers, and his boyfriend's wife opens the door. Audience members can not only see a woman, but also a child and a picture of the entire family on the wall facing the front door. This classic betrayal scene occurs in the queer community, and Lil Nas X's ability to portray these scenes is commendable. His use of visuals to perpetuate the notion that being gay is okay and natural is necessary in a society that still struggles to see LGBTQ members as equals, especially *Black* LGBTQ members. Elyssa Durham explains how "Black queer artists are fighting an intersectional battle: homophobic criticism from the Black community and racism from the LGBTQ community" (25). Lil Nas X brings both issues to the forefront and lives out his truth, hoping to expand an appreciation for the queer community, as well as the Black *and* queer community, by living his truth openly and expressing all areas of Black Queer Femme Bravado.

Finally, in the last scene, Lil Nas X is walking down the aisle in a wedding dress, holding a bouquet, something that most would think of a woman experiencing on her wedding day. He is breaking barriers of heteronormativity by not only being in a dress but also through his depiction of a gay wedding. When he gets to the end of the aisle however, the priest hands him a guitar, which he plays through the end of the song. This shift in demeanor portrays the struggles many in the LGBTQ community face: wanting to live a somewhat traditional life but being held back due to the suffocating heteronormative ideals in society. Lil Nas X uses his status and "the new media landscape to subvert typical systems of oppression LGBTQIA+ identities deal with in American society" (Thomas 4). Master's graduate student Emily Thomas expresses further,

> Lil Nas X's work has had a dramatic impact on the LGBTQIA+ community, as exemplified by the Trevor Project's decision to honour him with the 2021 "Suicide Prevention of the Year Award" due to his "openness about struggling with his sexuality," "advocacy around mental health issues" and "unapologetic celebration of his queer identity." (Thomas 4)

His ability to illustrate homosexuality in a way that is honest and relatable through his music videos is revolutionary and a key component of Black Queer Femme Bravado. Ultimately, Black Queer Femme Bravado exists to create spaces for queer voices to be heard, as well as allow queerness to exist openly within mainstream media.

Overall, Lil Nas X has not only empowered younger generations of LGBTQ youth to feel safe and comfortable in their skin, but he has also encouraged them to speak up for their rights as well. He "challenges and defies identity politics established in the Black community and hip-hop and showcases it on a mainstream platform" (Durham 27). In a society that functions primarily by those with power pushing their ideas and values on everyone else, allowing more queer artists into the music industry will begin to tip the scales of what people view as "acceptable" behavior. Furthermore, educating students on artists who break societal boundaries, who encourage minority voices to be heard, and who fight for the inclusion of all people creates safe classroom spaces. In her article "Dismantling Anti-Black Linguistic Racism in English Language Arts Classrooms: Toward an Anti-racist Black Language Pedagogy," April Baker-Bell contends that "when Black students' language practices are suppressed in classrooms or they begin to absorb messages that imply that BL is deficient, wrong, and unintelligent, this could cause them to internalize anti-Blackness and develop negative attitudes about their linguistic, racial, cultural, and intellectual identities and about themselves" (10). Including hip-hop music and promoting Black Queer Femme Bravado within the classroom encourages Black student language practices and supports a positive attitude toward Black communities, because teachers can support discussions around artists' specific content and how their wording and experiences are shaped from societal struggles. Those conversations can lead to short response papers and essays, allowing students to explain how marginalized people compartmentalize, cope with, and resist the deep-seated racism within American culture today. Not only is the inclusion of music that is primarily sought out by Black communities important to incorporate in classrooms, but also music that supports multiple "other" communities such as LGBTQIA+. With that being said, Lil Nas X is the perfect representative to use in order to reach multiple demographics and educate students on the vast complexities of language and the world. Classrooms are simply micro representations of society, especially in diverse areas; therefore, it becomes paramount to showcase a variety of beliefs, cultures, and backgrounds.

Notes

1. Grullon is an English instructor at Queensborough Community College.

2. The term *Straight Time* comes from José Esteban Muñoz's *Cruising Utopia*, combining meanings with Caroline Levine's definition of *rhythmic forms* as enduring and repeating across institutions. Straight Time is institutional, and some examples of experiences that are markers of queer time include having a crush, going to prom, getting married, etc.

Works Cited

Baker-Bell, April. "Dismantling Anti-Black Linguistic Racism in English Language Arts Classrooms: Toward an Anti-Racist Black Language Pedagogy." *Theory into Practice,* vol. 59, no. 1, 2019, pp. 8–21.

———. "We Been Knowin: Toward an Antiracist Language and Literacy Education." *Journal of Language and Literacy Education,* vol. 16, no. 1, 2020, pp. 1–12.

Banks, Adam. *Digital Griots: African American Rhetoric in a Multimedia Age.* Southern Illinois UP, 2011.

Durham, Elyssa. *Hip-Hop and Black Queer Defiance.* 2022. Grand Valley State University, MA thesis. https://scholarworks.gvsu.edu/gradprojects/109.

Grullon, Jaymi Leah. *Campy Musical Black Queer Forms: Finding Utopia in Lil Nas X's World of* MONTERO. 2022. St. John's College of Liberal Arts and Sciences, MA thesis. https://scholar.stjohns.edu/theses_dissertations/477.

Lil Nas X. "That's What I Want." *MONTERO,* Columbia Records, 2021. *iTunes* app.

McGee, Alexis. *Legacies of Womanhood in Blues and Hip Hop: A Critique of Feminism, Sonic Rhetoric, and Language.* 2018. The University of Texas at San Antonio, PhD dissertation. *Proquest,* https://www.proquest.com/docview/2090948625.

Pritchard, Eric Darnell. *Fashioning Lives: Black Queers and the Politics of Literacy.* Southern Illinois UP, 2016.

Royster, Jacqueline Jones. "Diversity and Writing: Dialogue within a Modern University." Proceedings; First Annual Conference. The Center for Interdisciplinary Studies of Writing, University of Minnesota, April 1990.

Smitherman, Geneva. *Black Talk: Words and Phrases from the Hood to the Amen Corner.* Houghton Mifflin, 1994.

Thomas, Emily. *Quare(-in) the Mainstream: Deconstructing New Media in Lil Nas X's* MONTERO. Goldsmiths, University of London, 2022. https://www.sonicscope.org/pub/wgczbm4b.

CHAPTER SEVEN

Digital Multimodal Composition (DMC) Engagement in English Language Classrooms: A Pakistani Perspective

ADEEL KHALID
Forman Christian College University & International Islamic University Islamabad

FAUZIA JANJUA
International Islamic University Islamabad

Writing has been one of the most critical and important aspects of a student's academic success (Crosthwaite, 2019). In today's digitalised world, newly admitted students in universities are already familiar with the art of communicating since an average adult has profiles on more than one social networking site (SNS), and many users synchronise specific types of material across several sites, from Twitter/X to Facebook, which they actively use and participate in. This participation in various digital platforms has also revolutionised the writing experiences that come mainly from writing on SNS like Instagram, WhatsApp, Facebook, Reddit, Snapchat, Twitter, etc. (Gee). Therefore, digital writing has been ubiquitous in students' lives. However, this writing type is mostly imperceptible to students and is not considered a part of any writing at all (Grabill and Hicks, 2005). This study, however, recognises the importance of digital writing by drawing inspiration from a study conducted by the Pew Internet and American Life Project, which considered digital writing as one of the essential components that provide an opportunity to expand students' digital literacies. Using social media also helps in connecting students to contexts outside of the classroom (Stewart). Digital writing holds significant importance and has been acknowledged by experts in the field and scholars around the world (Douglas and Vie).

The inclusion of Digital Multimodal Composing (DMC) in English as a Second Language (ESL) classrooms has emerged as a new genre of practice in academic writing, but little is known about how to develop and design a multimodal task for composing (Polio and Yoon). Research scholars in the pioneering studies of composition and computers argue that academic writers must be prepared for unique experiences in this digital world as the world is changing at a rapid pace, including experiences that we have never had (Hawisher and Selfe). These unique experiences involve writing and reading multimodal texts in today's digital communication. The writers have been reading and writing a wide selection of multimodal texts in the ESL context, such as blogs, websites, digital stories, electronic posters, digital timelines, video documentaries, podcasts, graphic novels, and PowerPoint slides. The study responds to the New London Group's 1996 concern that globalisation and technology have impacted students' literacy levels, necessitating an extended definition of literacy that emphasises the multimodal aspect of communication. In this paper, we attempt to examine students' writing practices and processes for composing an academic essay following academic requirements using writing and visual rubrics and to seek affordances in creating multimodal writing texts and how these digital spaces allow students potential for meaning-making beyond the out-of-date methods of teaching writing in an ESL Pakistani context. This research drew data from learners' authored and designed digital multimodal blogposts, including assignments, and teachers' assessments.

DMC in ESL Context

DMC refers to the practice of composing text using multiple modes such as writing, images, sounds, and videos (Ho). By integrating various modes, it allows for a more dynamic and engaging communication experience. This approach to composition has gained significant attention in recent years, particularly in the field of L2 writing. Research has begun to investigate the effects of DMC on unique features of L2 acquisition. With emerging technologies, especially during the pandemic and post-pandemic phases, these ESL academic writers have been engaged more than ever in producing complex multimodal texts for numerous audiences and purposes (Jiang). This presentation showcases how multimodal composing practices allow students to develop multiliteracy and creative skills as a multidisciplinary point for holistic student engagement. It introduces participants to digital instructional techniques and a range of technological tools to compose.

ESL Writing in Pakistan

Writing in Pakistan has been explored from various dimensions as academic writing needs to be appropriate language use with precision in structural exactness and communication skills (Mahboob and Elyas); however, teaching writing is undergoing a major shift, and with traditional writing pedagogy, it is not possible to equip university students to fully develop their digital literacy skills (Sajid and Siddiqui). Therefore, it is a pressing need for time to study how newly admitted students design their written texts and what affordances are allowed in their written texts. The skills and knowledge required for digital multimodal composition might be indicated by such expertise, which also has pedagogical implications for literacy instruction. This study attempts to fill this gap of acquiring and learning writing skills on digital spaces and platforms by exploring the students' conception of digital writing the impact that they construe on their academic performance and what affordances are allowed at the undergraduate writing program in Pakistan.

According to the World Bank, teachers and institutions ought to prepare students well with basic reading and writing yet develop students' digital literacy skills, as there is uncertainty about the kinds of skills the jobs of the future would require, while making the learners adapt to the latest market trends and demands. Learners need to be self-sufficient to write, infer and synthesise information, think critically, form opinions, be innovative, communicate well, and be resilient (*The Education Crisis*). The Higher Education Commission (HEC) of Pakistan's report on the Tertiary Education Sector Assessment also claims that written communication is one of the top ten soft skills lacking in fresh graduates (Mahmood). The HEC considers industry-university linkage significant to national and institutional progress because these institutions are considered key stakeholders in developing the required skills in the students. This university education at the undergraduate level plays a leading role in a knowledge-based economy and innovation. This derives from innovation, which is only possible via an industry-university long-run partnership (Bramwell and Wolfe). The World Economic Forum report asserts a change in higher educational institutions as past practices are insufficient in equipping students to compete in a challenging environment (Zahidi et al.). Overall Assessment of the Higher Education Sector Report finds that there is an inadequate institutional capacity to meet the rising demand for higher education with an increase in literacy level and growth enrollment (Mahmood). Universities in Pakistan need to make certain curriculum changes in their higher education institutions because writing is one such key skill that can enable students to project themselves, and through academic writing, these graduates can successfully present themselves in the job market.

Writing in Pakistani universities is taught mainly using traditional methods. Teachers and education administrators are often reluctant to accept new ways of digital writing as writing; rather, they call it blogging, netsurfing, and posting. Writing produced in social media contexts are not qualified to be included within the parameters of academic writing, and such writings are often called blog writing, chat, networking, conversation, etc. In terms of grammar, academic patterns, and assessment standards, these writings are not recognised as a significant part of students' writing lives. Composition researchers around the world are finding ways to incorporate this type of digital writing into the composition class for developing and promoting the required skills within an institutional framework as writing is the fundamental skill that can help students make an impact while presenting themselves in the job market.

Transfer Theory in ESL Writing while Teaching DMC

Learning how to write is a process that starts at a very early stage of a student's life and ends nowhere. So, the teachers who teach writing and composition need to take into consideration students' prior knowledge and practices that they are actively engaged in. Digital writing can serve as a specimen for engaging in writing across various disciplines and contexts. That is the reason why digital writing holds particular significance, and students frequently use these SNS platforms in their daily routines and a great deal of writing takes place on these SNS forums (Shepherd). According to Statista, Facebook has 2.80 billion users, followed by YouTube with 2.2 billion users and WhatsApp with two billion users in 2021. Pakistan is in eleventh place with 46.9 million users on Facebook. Some scholars assessed that 99% of college students use social networking sites for several other purposes (Junco).

Research Context

Research and scholarship in the field of writing have been explored from a theoretical and pedagogical point of view, but no study in Pakistan has studied the data from the perspectives of how students create alternate author paths using digital platforms and what affordances are privileged using these social media sites or how students perceive their writing and its connections to the composition that they study during their first year at the undergraduate level. This study focuses on the interaction between multimodality and one specific aspect of academic literacy—composing multimodal arguments. The multimodal argument genre serves as a tool for students to develop their critical thinking skills and become engaged members of society by negotiating and defending values (O'Halloran and Smith; Smith et al.). In this paper, we attempt to examine students' writing practices on composing an academic essay following academic requirements using writing and visuals and to seek affordances in creating multimodal writing texts, and how these digital spaces allow students potential for meaning-making beyond the out-of-date methods of teaching writing in ESL context (The New London Group). This study aims to study multimodal writings across social media platforms to see what affordances are allowed and can be part of formal writing and which form of writing is privileged over the others. The DMC as an intervention in a writing class to engage students in producing multimodal arguments in such forms as infographics and websites was employed to address student construction of multimodal arguments in this research.

Data for This Research

This data was analysed using qualitative and interpretive approaches. Consequently, the data analysis of this study was completed in principled iterative phases. In the formative phase, students produced DMCs through iterative rounds of coding. The emphasis was laid on multimodal analysis informed by Halliday (1993) and Kress and van Leeuwen (2020) on metafunctions. DMC blogs of the whole class were analysed based on their multimodal design choices and their rhetorical effects at the first stage. In the second stage, four students' works were analysed based on a similar analysis on DMC blog (Saldaña), guided by the metafunctions. At this stage the affordance of creating DMC among students was answered by analysing key students' DMC blogs, which included but were not limited to what themes they used for what post, landing pages, fonts and font changes, hashtags, background pictures, heading pictures, layout, and how they incorporated materials (linked, pasted, embedded) in their DMC blogs. This analysis comprised scrupulous examination of every DMC blogpost that students created, which we then analysed further through descriptive matrices to examine each element, using content analysis to analyse DMC blog, on the lookout for universal descriptors about them (Stewart). Through these evaluations, researchers were able to gain a better understanding of how students utilized the platforms for producing their DMC blogs and the multimodal affordance employed and potential digital affordance therein.

Analytical Dimensions for This Study

While conceptualising with multiple modes, learners stated how using pictures, music, and films assisted them in conceptualizing literary topics. Meaning-making through nonlinguistic modes frequently came before learners' written notes or additional textual components of their DMC projects, giving them a thematic basis on which to build their analyses. Via visual conceptualization, learners worked together to establish the analytical framework for their DMC projects in an ESL context. These procedures entailed using abstract terms (e.g., "culture" and "identity") to search for images on the internet. After that, learners visually brainstormed by looking at and evaluating a number of the photographs that their searches turned up. Discussions and links to the themes in the books they were studying were stimulated by these viewings. Many learners described how they used visuals as a starting point for their literary assessments. Before they started writing, several learners multimodally imagined ideas by watching videos or listening to music. Learners were also able to "see" the information by conceptualizing through visual and auditory modes, which encouraged them to develop a sensory comprehension of the book. Several learner replies repeated this pattern of using multimodal composition to "visualize" text. Learners described how engaging with the material in more than one form forced them to think creatively and to be less literal in their initial readings. Further analyses for this research drew on the "design and structure of CFRIDiL" by Sindoni et al. (45). The descriptors intend to answer specific questions within European contexts, including multimodal orchestration, technology, intercultural communication. and transversal skills for adopting, developing. and assessing digital multimodal texts as academic genre texts.

Implication of the Study

This study is significant as it contributes to the existing body of literature within the field of rhetoric and composition, which is an emerging domain in Pakistani education and linguistic landscape. This study helps to germinate a new scholarly dimension toward teaching writing skills with the use of social media networks and informs the curriculum developers and designers to keep the role of digital literacies and this research as part of the development of digital multiliteracy scholarship in Pakistan. Though originated as a Western legacy, digital composition, as noted by Eyman, can be a discipline that is flexible not only in terms of methodology but also in terms of its application across Pakistani cultural contexts. This research showcased how digital multimodal composing practices allow students to develop multiliteracy using digital affordances and creative skills as a multidisciplinary point for holistic student engagement. Such digital practices and pedagogies encouraged learners and practitioners to position themselves in digital spaces while using digital instructional techniques and a range of technological tools to compose several genres of writing that are translingual, transdisciplinary, and transnational.

Works Cited

Bramwell, Allison, and David A. Wolfe. "Universities and Regional Economic Development: The Entrepreneurial University of Waterloo." *Research Policy*, vol. 37, no. 8, 2008, pp. 1175–87.

Crosthwaite, Peter Robert. "Definite Article Bridging Relations in L2: A Learner Corpus Study." *Corpus Linguistics and Linguistic Theory*, vol. 15, no. 2, 2019, pp. 297–319.

Eyman, Douglas. *Digital Rhetoric: Theory, Method, Practice*. U of Michigan P, 2015.

Gee, James Paul. "The New Literacy Studies." *The Routledge Handbook of Literacy Studies,* edited by Jennifer Rowsell and Kate Pahl, Routledge, 2015, pp. 35–48.

Grabill, Jeffrey T., and Troy Hicks. "Multiliteracies Meet Methods: The Case for Digital Writing in English Education." *English Education,* vol. 37, no. 4, 2005, pp. 301–11.

Halliday, Michael AK. "Towards a Language-Based Theory of Learning." *Linguistics and Education,* vol. 5, no. 2, 1993, pp. 93–116.

Hawisher, Gail E., and Cynthia L. Selfe, eds. *Passions, Pedagogies, and 21st Century Technologies.* Utah State UP, 1999.

Ho, Wing Yee Jenifer. "The Construction of Translanguaging Space through Digital Multimodal Composing: A Case Study of Students' Creation of Instructional Videos." *Journal of English for Academic Purposes,* vol. 58, 2022. https://doi.org/10.1016/j.jeap.2022.101134.

Jiang, Lianjiang. "Digital Multimodal Composing and Investment Change in Learners' Writing in English as a Foreign Language." *Journal of Second Language Writing,* vol. 40, June 2018, pp. 60–72. https://doi.org/10.1016/j.jslw.2018.03.002.

Junco, Reynol. "Too Much Face and Not Enough Books: The Relationship between Multiple Indices of Facebook Use and Academic Performance." *Computers in Human Behavior,* vol. 28, no. 1, 2012, pp. 187–98.

Kress, Gunther, and Theo van Leeuwen. *Reading Images: The Grammar of Visual Design.* Routledge, 2020.

Mahboob, Ahmar, and Tariq Elyas. "English in the Kingdom of Saudi Arabia." *World Englishes,* vol. 33, no. 1, 2014, pp. 128–42.

Mahmood, Khalid. "Higher Education Commission Pakistan." Higher Education Commission (HEC) (2016).

O'Halloran, Kay L., and Bradley A. Smith. "Multimodal Studies." *Multimodal Studies: Exploring Issues and Domains,* Routledge, 2012, pp. 21–34.

Polio, Charlene, and Hyung-Jo Yoon. "Exploring Multi-Word Combinations as Measures of Linguistic Accuracy in Second Language Writing." *Learner Corpus Research Meets Second Language Acquisition,* edited by Bert Le Bruyn and Magali Paquot, Cambridge UP, 2021, pp. 96–121.

Sajid, Muhammad, and Jawaid Ahmed Siddiqui. "Lack of Academic Writing Skills in English Language at Higher Education Level in Pakistan: Causes, Effects and Remedies." *International Journal of Language and Linguistics,* vol. 2, no. 4, 2015, pp. 174–86.

Saldaña, Johnny. *The Coding Manual for Qualitative Researchers.* SAGE, 2021.

Shepherd, Ryan P. "Digital Writing, Multimodality, and Learning Transfer: Crafting Connections between Composition and Online Composing." *Computers and Composition,* vol. 48, June 2018, pp. 103–114. https://doi.org/10.1016/j.compcom.2018.03.001.

Sindoni, Maria Grazia, et al. "The Common Framework of Reference for Intercultural Digital Literacies." EU-MADE4LL, European Multimodal and Digital Education for Language Learning. https://www.eumade4ll.eu/wp-content/uploads/2019/09/cfridil-framework-MG3_IM_4-compresso.pdf

Smith, Blaine E. "Composing across Modes: A Comparative Analysis of Adolescents' Multimodal Composing Processes." *Learning, Media and Technology,* vol. 42, no. 3, 2017, pp. 259–78.

———. "Mediational Modalities." *Research in the Teaching of English,* vol. 53, no. 3, 2019, pp. 197–222.

Smith, Michael W., et al. "The Common Core: New Standards, New Teaching." *Phi Delta Kappan,* vol. 94, no. 8, 2013, pp. 45–48.

Stewart, Olivia G. "A Critical Review of the Literature of Social Media's Affordances in the Classroom." *E-Learning and Digital Media,* vol. 12, no. 5–6, 2015, pp. 481–501.

Walls, Douglas M., and Stephanie Vie, eds. *Social Writing/Social Media: Publics, Presentations, and Pedagogies.* WAC Clearinghouse, 2017.

World Bank. "The Education Crisis: Being in School Is Not the Same as Learning." (2019).

Zahidi, Saadia, et al. "The Future of Jobs Report 2020." World Economic Forum, 2020. https://www.weforum.org/reports/the-future-of-jobs-report-2020.

CHAPTER EIGHT

Writing beyond Campus: Reflecting Critically on Abundant, Local Communal Knowledge

NOAH PATTERSON
Purdue University

JACQUELINE BORCHERT
Purdue University

NATHAN MCBURNETT
Purdue University

Writing centers have a long history of community engagement, and many centers now make this a central part of their mission and daily operations (LeCluyse et al.). Throughout the twenty-first century, writing centers and universities have employed an emerging critical framework of community engagement that problematizes more traditional approaches to the work. In response to a history of thorny relationships between universities and their surrounding communities—including individuals, nonprofit service providers, political or labor organizations, schools, neighborhood associations, small businesses, cultural and arts institutions, mutual aid organizations, and more—critical service-learning attempts to disrupt colonial, positivist, paternalistic, and monocultural tendencies that have characterized many universities' approaches to developing community partnerships (Clegorne; LaDousa 38; Mehta et al. 86; Mitchell; Rajah 2–4; Shumer 79, 81). Engaging with community work at our own center, located within an R1, public, Midwestern university, we have been conducting a writing-based needs assessment with local community organizations to determine opportunities for collaboration between our unit and the surrounding community beyond campus. With a focus on the work of writing centers, this article briefly outlines key differences between traditional and critical service-learning, posits critical reflection as a tool for community-university partnerships, and advocates for the inclusion of local knowledge to lean in to a partnership's critical and justice-oriented potential.

Critical Service-Learning

Critical service-learning (CSL) is a model that prioritizes equitable, mutually beneficial relationships with community partners that focus on challenging existing systems of power and resource distribution (Mitchell 53). While traditional service-learning tends to emphasize the potential scholarly benefits for students and faculty, CSL shifts the emphasis to building "authentic relationships" in the community to cultivate a sense of "social responsibility" and address "critical community issues" (Mitchell 51; Zastoupil & Sarmiento 169). In essence, CSL then becomes a "problem-solving instrument for political and social reform" where students are encouraged to act as "agents of social change" in service of community justice (Fenwick 6; Mitchell 51–52). To do this, CSL often takes the form of community-engaged projects founded on the qualities of mutuality, equity, respectability, and co-defined goals and objectives.

Scholars argue that CSL promotes complex thinking and reasoning skills among students (Wang and Rodgers). Writing exercises such as critical reflection are especially important because they provide a means by which students can actively analyze and address their own perspectives within the context of social justice work. At our own center, we have promoted a model of critical reflection that emphasizes *action* within the context of service work. By emphasizing both reflection and action, critical reflection can support existing service-learning pedagogy across disciplines by challenging students to both interrogate and improve their approach to community-engaged projects.

Critical Reflection

In order to authentically engage with service-learning in ways that honor the local context, active employment of critical reflection within the classroom allows for a more equitable and purposeful experience for both students and communities. To truly ground ourselves in cultural abundance and the abundance of the local community, students must reflect on the knowledge in an active and periodic way through critical reflection that explores the intersection of experience, discussions, reading, theory, and practice. Critical reflections act as a tool to assess student learning and establish personal, classroom, and community knowledge into conversation through various lenses and at different levels. Discussing the active role students must take in their growth, Kemmis argues, "We are inclined to think of reflection as something quiet and personal. The argument here is that reflection is action-oriented, social and political. Its 'product' is praxis (informed, committed action) and the most eloquent and socially significant form of human action" (139). Despite many who think of reflection as simple busywork and superficial, the act of critical reflection generates, deepens, and documents learning through evidence-based, integrative, analytical actions such as confronting bias, discovering causality, challenging superficial conclusions, and producing a tangible expression of new understandings for feedback. It reinforces and amplifies reflection within the local, historical, and global context that extends the experience to individual and societal futures.

Critical reflections are key to process the learning that is inherent in these community-engaged scholarship and service-learning experiences. University stakeholders are at constant risk of approaching partnerships with an unintentionally colonialist approach, failing to actively make sure the reciprocal relationship is balanced. The pedagogical benefits of incorporating critical reflections into the classroom are vast. Critical reflections become sites for students to draw connections between their own funds of knowledge and those they encounter in the community. Furthermore, within the requirements of academic life, instructors can measure the abstract benefits of community-engaged work, using the critical reflections as vehicles to guide and assess student learning.

Additionally, critical reflection spurs the participant to identify tacit knowledge as well as gaps, deepening professional values and understandings of complex concepts. True critical reflection is not a linear process. It is instead composed of cycles. The primary cycles move between inward reflection, outward reflection, and exploratory reflection. All three of these are deeply intertwined and affected by the others, hence the cyclical relationship. There are many well-known strategies for achieving this thinking (the most famous being the *What? So what? Now what?* model) that instructors and individuals can employ to guide them through this loop of reflection and maximize future transferable knowledge (Rolfe et al.).

Centering Local Knowledge

As students critically reflect on their community-engaged work, instructors should ensure students seek and value the local knowledge inherent in the community to avoid paternalistic approaches. Allahwala et al.'s study examines their participatory action research collaboration between City Studies students and the Kingston-Galloway/Orton Park (KGO) community in Toronto. The authors note student presentations would identify issues such as exposed power lines as "reasons" community members were not invested in their own safety; however, senior community members indicated the site had been reported, but no one had fixed it (14–15). As a result, community engagement initiatives that do not consider local knowledge "run the risk of re-inscribing existing hierarchies of knowledge and power differentials, especially when the university and university students are seen as being in a position to 'fix' the problem in the community" (18).

While students should seek and value local knowledge, building these networks can be difficult; as Mehta et al. note, academic institutions often view indigenous or local knowledge frameworks "with skepticism, if not contempt" (90). However, Marcus Chilaka's study surveyed dozens of health experts about their experiences seeking knowledge from local community members when designing health interventions. About two-thirds of practitioners (65.5%) indicated that collecting this knowledge was "easy" (57.4%) or "very easy" (8.1%) and a vast majority (98.4%) called this data "useful" (36.1%) or "very useful" (62.3%) (104). To foster these connections in mutual and equitable ways, "the community engagement process must continue to be developed and refined in order to strengthen the utility of local knowledge" (Chilaka 108). This constant refinement also ensures the project is responsive to the fluid needs of all partners and contributions from community members. One way to facilitate this refinement is through "a reflection of *process*" rather than "output," something our critical reflection framework hopes to facilitate through exploring inward, outward, and exploratory reflective "levels" (Allahwala et al. 18, emphasis original).

Using these inward, outward, and exploratory levels allow writers to consider project impact and refine their process in ways that expand reflective practice beyond personal experience. Inward reflection begins with this individual experience, asking writers to consider how the experience impacted them. Writers may consider the skills they have gained, what they have learned about themselves, assumptions that have been challenged, or potential revisions to the project they will enact moving forward. Outward reflection considers the experience's impact on other individual community members. Here, writers should remark on observable impacts on others, whether or not these impacts were intended, and unanticipated outcomes. Additionally, outward reflection should explore impact in terms of the collective. In other words, reflections should explore the local circumstances that necessitated the project, how the project or experience responded to that local context, and the short- and long-term implications of the experience on the community. This can be expanded to societal levels, conceptualizing how these local circumstances are informed by broader, systemic factors, and whether the project addresses the symptoms or sources of these issues. Finally, at the exploratory level, impact is considered more broadly for the purpose of assessment and refinement of processes. Writers can determine the metrics used to assess impact and where the project held the most impact—whether at personal, individual, organizational, local, or societal levels. This comprehensive reflective practice ensures writers consider project output *and* their process, situating their reflection as a space to respond to that process and consider required changes that emphasize mutuality, equity, and valuation of local knowledge.

Ultimately, writing centers are uniquely positioned to advocate for indigenous and local knowledges as institutional spaces involved in writing across the disciplines, members of community-university partnerships, and proponents of other justice-oriented pedagogies, like linguistic justice. As such, writing centers can put this theory into practice and lead by example to affirm the argument that "universities should be able to trust local people to contribute useful knowledge, which can be evident by their lived experience" to establish "strategic channels and targeted partnerships for knowledge production or exchange" (Mbah 18). As the authors of this paper continue to assess the needs of our own writing center and our local community—within the context of writing and as advocates for critical reflection in the classroom—we hope to take our project further by connecting directly with the community members that local social service organizations seek to support. Though this work is complex and the researchers imperfect, by employing the ideals held in this article, we hope to push other writing centers to critically reflect on their institutional contexts and find ways to approach and execute service-learning in more equitable and mutually beneficial ways.

Works Cited

Allahwala, Ahmed, et al. "Empowering Communities or Reproducing Stereotypes: Negotiating Power and Knowledge in Service-Learning Involving Youth." *Currents in Teaching & Learning,* vol. 7, no. 1, Fall 2014, pp. 6–22. https://search.ebscohost.com/login.aspx?direct=true&AuthType=sso&db=eue&AN=101595961&site=ehost-live&custid=purdue.

Chilaka, Marcus A. "Drawing from the Well of Community Participation: An Evaluation of the Utility of Local Knowledge in the Health Impact Assessment Process." *Community Development,* vol. 46, no. 2, Mar. 2015, pp. 100–10. https://doi.org/10.1080/15575330.2015.1014060.

Clegorne, Nicholas. "'Here We Come to Save the Day': Exploring the Dark Side of Servant Leadership Narratives among College Freshmen." *Journal of Curriculum Theorizing,* vol. 31, no. 2, 2016, pp. 33–44. ProQuest, https://www.proquest.com/scholarly-journals/here-we-come-save-day-exploring-dark-side-servant/docview/1827601001/se-2.

Fenwick, Tara J. *Experiential Learning: A Theoretical Critique from Five Perspectives.* Information Series No. 385. Publications, Center on Education and Training for Employment, 1900 Kenny Road, Columbus, OH 43210-1090, 2001. ERIC, https://eric.ed.gov/?id=ED454418.

Kemmis, Stephen. "Action Research and the Politics of Reflection." *Reflection: Turning Experience into Learning,* edited by David Boud Walker and David Rosemary Keogh, Routledge, 2013, pp. 139–63. https://doi.org/10.4324/9781315059051.

LaDousa, Chaise. "'Everyone's Got Room to Grow': A Discourse Analysis of Service-Learning Rhetoric in Higher Education." *Learning and Teaching,* vol. 6, no. 2, 2013, pp. 33–52.

LeCluyse, Christopher, et al. "Write Here, Right Now: Shifting a Community Writing Center from a Place to a Practice." *Community Literacy Journal,* vol. 15, no. 1, Apr. 2021, https://doi.org/10.25148/CLJ.15.1.009368.

Mbah, Marcellus. "Can Local Knowledge Make the Difference? Rethinking Universities' Community Engagement and Prospect for Sustainable Community Development." *Journal of Environmental Education,* vol. 50, no. 1, Jan. 2019, pp. 11–22. EBSCOhost, https://doi.org/10.1080/00958964.2018.1462136.

Mehta, Khanjan, et al. "AcademIK Connections: Bringing Indigenous Knowledge and Perspectives into the Classroom." *Journal of Community Engagement & Scholarship,* vol. 6, no. 2, Dec. 2013, pp. 83–91. https://doi.org/10.54656/xlux1060.

Mitchell, Tania D. "Traditional vs. Critical Service-Learning: Engaging the Literature to Differentiate Two Models." *Michigan Journal of Community Service Learning,* vol. 14 , no. 2, 2008, pp. 50–65. https://eric.ed.gov/?redir=http%3a%2f%2fquod.lib.umich.edu%2fm%2fmjcsl%2fim ages%2f3239521.0014.205.pdf.

Rajah, Surversperi Suryakumari. "Conceptualising Community Engagement through the Lens of African Indigenous Education." *Perspectives in Education,* vol. 37, no. 1, June 2019, pp. 1–14. EBSCOhost, https://doi.org/10.18820/2519593X/pie.v37i1.1.

Rolfe, Gary, et al. *Critical Reflection for Nursing and the Helping Professions: A User's Guide.* Palgrave Macmillan, 2001.

Shumer, Rob. "Science or Storytelling: How Should We Conduct and Report Service-Learning Research?" *Michigan Journal of Community Service Learning,* vol. Special Issue, no. 1, Fall 2000, pp. 76–83. http://hdl.handle.net/2027/spo.3239521.spec.110.

Wang, Yan, and Robert Rodgers. "Impact of Service-Learning and Social Justice Education on College Students' Cognitive Development." *NASPA Journal,* vol. 43, no. 2, July 2006, pp. 316–37. Taylor and Francis+NEJM, https://doi.org/10.2202/1949-6605.1642.

Zastoupil, Garret, and Carolina Sarmiento. "Service-Learning, Rights to the City, and Justice in Community Practitioner Preparation." *Journal of Community Practice,* vol. 30, May 2022, pp. 1–12. ResearchGate, https://doi.org/10.1080/10705422.2022.2070315.

CHAPTER NINE

Ethos *in the Age of AI*

PEGEEN REICHERT POWELL
Aurora University

ChatGPT exploded onto the educational scene in the middle of the 2022–2023 academic year. Very few people were prepared. As a dean of a college that houses humanities, business, and the social and behavioral sciences in a Hispanic-serving institution, I observed a myriad of responses, from the marketing faculty eager to teach their students prompt engineering to English faculty urging more reliance on Turnitin; from history faculty contemplating the return of Bluebook exams to the visual artist excited about the possibilities for creative production. Will it be the death of original thinking? Or a boon to students, especially those required to perform in a language other than their first language? What is more important, staying on top of the academic integrity issues or addressing the problems of unequal access to a technology that will likely shape the future of many careers? Since the initial furor about ChatGPT, the discourse has become more subdued, but no less urgent, and questions from the mundane to the existential surrounding AI and large language model (LLM) chatbots like ChatGPT continue to circulate throughout higher education.[1]

I argue that among the various resources composition studies and communication specialists can draw on, the rich and robust concept of *ethos* provides a heuristic for thinking about how we might respond to ChatGPT and other AI, and for teaching students to navigate the tricky intellectual and ethical landscape of AI. As we consider some of the central concepts and tenets of our field that could be upended by LLMs—authorship and audience, process and product, the personal and political nature of writing—we recognize that our field necessarily values the tension between seemingly opposing ideas. *Ethos* allows us to maintain some productive tension as we think through the implications of our students, indeed of everyone, using chatbots in their writing.

In surveying the dominant theories of ethos, James S. Baumlin and Craig A. Meyer argue that any model of ethos "orients itself from (and, in so doing, privileges) one of the three perspectives: that of self, or of culture, or of language" (4). As a (disembodied?) text-generator, AI chatbots would seem to invoke a theory of ethos that privileges language over self and culture:

> within such a model, the self-expressive self "dissolves" within the interstices of texts. Following Jacques Derrida (1930–2004), deconstructionists declare writing's primacy over speech: "orphaned" from the living, embodied voice of the speaker, the written text confesses its loss of authorial presence. . . . Within such a model, one cannot say that the self "textualizes" itself: that, after all, would posit the speaking/writing subject as a point of origin whose existence precedes language. (5)

The "self" of a chatbot like ChatGPT or Google Gemini seems to dissolve into the text it produces; there is no "self" that exists outside of the response to an interlocutor's prompt.

However, Baumlin and Meyer seek not to resolve the tensions among the three perspectives—the focus on self, culture, or language—but rather to sustain the tensions as a way to position the concept of ethos "in/for the Twenty-First Century" as the title of their piece declares. They point to Nedra Reynolds, who notes that ethos "shifts and changes over time, across texts, and around competing spaces" (qtd. in Baumlin and Meyer, 3). What Baumlin and Meyer do in their genealogical study of ethos is give "each side a fair hearing," and they leave "readers to choose *which* version/s of ethos serve in *which* times and places within *which* specific exigencies before *which* specific audiences" (3). For my purposes here, the slash in "version/s" is most important, the implication that there may be multiple versions of ethos, foci on self, culture, and language, at once in a given writing situation. What matters is sustaining the tension among self, culture, and language as we approach writing with AI.

Likewise, in developing the concept of *cyberethos* by fusing the Aristotelian concept of *ethos* with cybernetics, Kristie S.

Fleckenstein argues that "*ethos* morphs across borders, resisting all efforts to hold it stable" (5). Helpfully, Fleckenstein raises the issue of ethics in this context: "If we have no stable boundaries, no stable reality, and no stable subject, how do we judge whose 'voice,' as well as whose reality, resonates with the greatest ethical authority, the greatest 'good character'?" (5). For Fleckenstein, cyberethos requires us to attend to an "ecological ethics" (5). Ethics is not solely located in the material world, but in a living system comprised of the discourse, the body in front of the screen, and the identity created on the screen, in what she refers to as "the feedback/feedforward phenomenon of cyberethos" (9). The instability of the environment in which we write online, using AI or not, is not a reason to abandon considerations of ethics, but a reason to multiply the locations where we must marry good character with good action.

How, then, might we use this concept to approach conversations with our students, colleagues, and the industry folks who are moving full steam ahead with AI applications? Perhaps the most frequent, even if for some of us not the most urgent, question we hear is about academic integrity. There are concerns that there is no way to "catch" a student who uses a chatbot on an assignment, because the text has been generated using an LLM, and so what is produced is new, rather than copied from a source one might identify with Turnitin or a Google search. A plagiarism case framed in these terms sees the author as an autonomous actor and the text as either produced by that author or produced by someone else. Right or wrong.

The concept of ethos certainly doesn't allow us to abandon questions of right or wrong. However, it may no longer be a binary choice, if it ever was. The writer who uses a chatbot is both author and audience, an interlocutor with the code that turns a vast hidden database of language use into prose. The chatbot is part of the writer's process and also turns out part (if not all) of the product. The writer is a person, with all of the ethical, social, and political implications that personhood entails, who "owns" the text when they put their name on it and hand it in. And that text is also embedded in the ethical, social, and political realities of the online texts it draws from, the cultures in which the author lives, and the classroom context in which it is being evaluated. Questions of good character and good action in this messy writing situation multiply, and we must hold the answers to those questions in a state of tension.

In fact, perhaps answers to those questions isn't the point. Rather, teaching students to raise the questions in the first place may be the point. Instead of asking "Did you or did you not write this paper?" we might ask questions such as "What do you know about the database from which the chatbot draws? Have you considered whether or not the database is infused with the injustices that exist everywhere online? What counts as good character in this classroom? In your culture? In your future career? Do you believe that this text is a manifestation of good character? Is it a manifestation of good action?" Questions about ethos like these necessarily open up much deeper and broader lines of inquiry. Those questions and the subsequent inquiry become the process; the product produced by the chatbot becomes an occasion for writing-to-learn.

In short, ethos provides a way for us to talk with the students who come through our writing classrooms, as well as our colleagues in a variety of disciplines, about the ethical implications of writing in the age of LLMs. These implications go far beyond questions of academic integrity, even if that is the most obvious. Ethos is at once accessible and a concept for "writing abundance," and like the 2024 CCCC conference theme calls on us to do, ethos also demands that we pay attention to the different material, social, and political places from which we and our students write. Following the lead of Baumlin, Meyer, Reynolds, and Fleckenstein, we must expand our considerations beyond the text that the chatbot generates, to questions about the "self" of the post-human subject as well as to the cultures in which the text is received, including the ways that different disciplines and professions might read that self.

Note

1. I have neither the space nor expertise to explain how large language models and chatbots that rely on them work. Perhaps the best bibliography that I have found for writing professionals on the subject

of AI in general as it pertains to writing instruction has been compiled by Anna Mills: https://wac.colostate.edu/repository/collections/ai-text-generators-and-teaching-writing-starting-points-for-inquiry/.

Works Cited

Baumlin, James S., and Craig A. Meyer. "Positioning Ethos in/for the Twenty-First Century: An Introduction to Histories of Ethos." *Humanities,* vol. 7, no. 78, 2018, pp. 3–26.

Fleckenstein, Kristie S. "Cybernetics, Ethos, and Ethics: The Plight of the Bread-and-Butter-Fly." *Plugged In: Technology, Rhetoric and Culture in a Posthuman Age,* edited by Lynn Worsham and Gary A. Olson, Hampton Press, 2008, pp. 3–23.

CHAPTER TEN

Reclaiming Latinx Rhetorics: Teaching Archival Research Writing to Spotlight Abundance in Students' Funds of Knowledge and Rhetorical Inheritances

LORETTA VICTORIA RAMIREZ
California State University, Long Beach

This study considers student-led archival retrieval projects wherein learners explore meaningful rhetorical antecedents that reflect student abundance. Situating my pedagogy, I teach composition and rhetoric in a Chicano and Latino Studies department at California State University, Long Beach. In this context, I have restructured writing courses to centralize marginalized rhetorical histories, chiefly historical Latinx rhetorics, since my class demographics are predominately Latinx. However, students also consider underrepresented rhetorics, including Indigenous, American Indian, African American, Asian American and Pacific Islander, transcultural, transnational, intersectional, LGBTQIA+, two-spirit, feminist, disability, and working-class rhetorics. To ethically address de-centered voices, I envision the teaching of cultural rhetorics as reanimating historical communicative traditions into students' living embodied identities and agendas. This plan nurtures discursive spaces that validate students' ethnic-academic identities so they might practice rhetorical sovereignty in modes, styles, and languages that best advance student goals (see Lyons). These efforts manifest in first-year composition, a new upper-division research methodology course (*Archival Quest: Reclaiming Latinx Rhetorics*) that I created, and an existing *History of Chicano Rhetoric* course that I redesigned based on notions of *hauntology as homecoming*. Consistent throughout my three courses, students practice writing that advances epistemological freedoms and makes apparent abundance in students' funds of knowledge (for *epistemological freedoms*, see Ndlovu-Gatsheni; *funds of knowledge*, see Gonzalez et al.).

The Three-Course Archival Research Sequence

Starting in fall 2020, I employed archival studies to satisfy my composition courses' institutionally mandated research paper. In summer 2021, I collaborated with cross-departmental composition colleagues to design a one-year stretch pedagogy that I later tailored for my department to centralize Latinx archival research. I found that stretch composition accommodates rigorous, time-intensive primary research skill-building while ongoing focus on archival projects fortifies the two-term cohesion. Since I teach in an ethnic studies department wherein students primarily identify as Latinx, I respond to students demonstrating desire for validation as undergraduates and inheritors of Latinx rhetorical lineages isolated from central narratives. Accordingly, I join scholars such as Pamela VanHaitsma, Wendy Hayden, Jessica Enoch, and James P. Purdy, who practice archival writing, research, and cataloging pedagogies in composition, yet I bridge into ethnic studies and decolonial theory. My courses observe "other faces" of the Americas, representing rhetorical histories beyond mainstays (see Baca and Villanueva). Concurrently, students consider *delinking* rhetorical practices from privileged forms of semiotic and epistemological systems (see Mignolo; Ruiz and Sánchez; García and Cortez). Below is the stretch composition assignment overview.

- ◆ Term One
  - Literacy narrative exploring emotions of centrality (or lack of) in universities.

- Counterstory responding to *myth of self* by assembling self-identified discursive community via primary sources.
- Portfolio curating multimodal archive of self.

◆ Term Two
- Archival Rhetoric Research Paper investigating archival antecedent(s) whose inventions resonate with learner's curiosities, ambitions, and/or assertions of rhetorical sovereignty.
- Autoethnography constructing knowledge of self and culture to support epistemological freedoms.
- Portfolio curating multimodal archive of self.

In my *Archival Quest* course, students analyze correlations between historical concealments and values placed on lives (see Martinez 409). I moderate discussions on *symbolic annihilation* as deriving from archival underrepresentation and producing historical erasures and classroom unbelonging (see Caswell et al. 58–59). *Archival Quest* interrogates power dynamics that shape institutionalized archives and encourages students to expand notions of *archives* from libraries to living environments. Students research family cupboards, garages, neighborhood parks, sidewalks, businesses, and community centers. Some consider their bodies, studying tattoos, piercings, scars, grooming, and (dis) abilities. Pivoting into one's lived/living artifacts positions students to assume responsibility as knowledge curators and constructors. Indeed, many perform archival-based autoethnographies to first centralize self (the *auto*biographical element), then explore one's culture (*ethno*), and articulate lived experiences through research that contextualizes solution-seeking as relevant to society and academia (*graphy*). By employing archival-based autoethnographies, students magnify the abundance accumulated in body and memory as original contributions to academia and community. While I have published on *Archival Quest* (see the author's "Archival Quest") and composition (see the author's "Digging the Archives"), here I focus on *History of Chicano Rhetoric*, wherein I implement thematic pedagogy that I call *hauntology as homecoming*.

History of Chicano Rhetoric

To study cultural rhetorics is to often search for voices mitigated by historical disconnections and thereby identified in sometimes spectral ambiguities. Hence, a prevailing endeavor in my *History of Chicano Rhetoric* course is to investigate what has been disrupted from mainstream legibility. Students consider phantom voices suppressed through neglect, violence, and politicized erasures. We "listen to ghosts," recalling Malea Powell's tactics to recover ancestorial rhetorics and epistemologies contained therein. As Powell writes, listening to ghosts unearths stories that arise "from the mess of blood and bones upon which 'America' is literally built, but also those rooted in other knowledges, other ways of knowing, other ways of being and becoming that frequently go unheard and unsaid in much scholarly work" (12).

The *History of Chicano Rhetoric* course highlights impacts of history on emotions of belonging. Students consider Michelle Ballif's *historiography as hauntology,* a methodological process where scholars embark on historical probes that focus attention on suppressed narratives. Ballif asserts historians' ethical obligation to listen to what is unfamiliar yet leaves us restless (145). It is important to note that restlessness for some historians and student researchers stems from the unfamiliarity of their cultural rhetorics within daily academic engagements. In my ethnic studies writing classes, hauntings open occasions to (re)animate rhetorical inheritances into immediate embodied purposes. Hauntings beckon rhetorical homecoming. Ancestors guide rhetorics into emotions of belonging.

As such, I shape pedagogy that I call *hauntology as homecoming,* which introduces students to Latinx historical and living rhetorics so students might locate, assess, and participate in their abundance. We consider how this abundance shapes academic voices that are often historically disconnected from cultural rhetorics. Accordingly, these are the learning outcomes in *hauntology as homecoming*:

- ◆ Define cultural rhetorics as an encompassing field while personally and socially accounting for rhetorical (un)belonging within obscured human cultures.

- ◆ Examine (un)settled pasts to stimulate methodological expansions and ethical reasoning.
- ◆ Compose a researched creative advocacy paper that centralizes civic and cultural knowledge-making.

The course's final project asks students to offer their living voices as mediums for the silenced. Verbalizing buried rhetorics, now recontextualized in immediate conditions and moments, students provide homecoming in their bodies for historical rhetorics and locate homecoming for themselves as they assert belonging in practices chosen from rhetorical options. This task is presented as a creative advocacy project crafted to support contemporary issues while mindful of abundant cultural rhetorics at students' bidding. Examples include recorded speeches, letters, opinion columns, poster boards with accompanying statements of purpose, documentary scripts, advocacy websites, and social media campaigns.

Recently, a student produced an illustrated children's book on microaggressions in an eighth-grade classroom after examining twenty-five years of Pura Belpré Award recipients. The award honors Latinx children's literature writers and illustrators who best portray, affirm, and celebrate Latinx cultural experiences. While the student's study of historical rhetorics stemmed as recently as the 1990s, her project epitomizes learning goals to define a cultural rhetoric by employing it as a vehicle to address rhetorical (un)belonging, mobilize methodological expansions and ethical reasonings, and compose a researched creative advocacy project that centralizes civic and cultural knowledge-making. My student, a major in the School of Education's Integrated Teacher Education program, selected voice, style, and medium to advance a narrative that centralizes her culture, views, and goals to serve as a K–12 teacher.

Final Thoughts

In ongoing projects to make legible violently silenced rhetorics, my students find assistance from Gesa Kirsch, Romeo García, Caitlin Burns Allen, and Walker P. Smith's *Unsettling Archival*

Research. Kirsch and colleagues *unsettle the settled* to expose "modern/colonial universities" as "wounded/ing and haunted/ing spaces and places" wherein "colonial violence, slavery, systemic and epistemic racism, and policing and police brutality [are kept] open and alive" (5). My scholarship also concerns rhetorical woundedness as an insistent marker that many students remain historically disconnected from living realities due to epistemic racism in curricula and learning materials (see the author's *The Wound and the Stitch*). Inspired by Walter Mignolo's *pluriverse*, I support regenerating historical genealogies to accommodate multitudes of rhetorical lineages identified by student abundance. I believe *hauntology as homecoming* could advance *pluriversalities* in colonized, diasporic, and marginalized populations.

Works Cited

Baca, Damián, and Víctor Villanueva, eds. *Rhetorics of the Americas: 3114 BCE to 2012 CE*. Palgrave, 2010.

Ballif, Michelle. "Historiography as Hauntology: Paranormal Investigations into the History of Rhetoric." *Theorizing Histories of Rhetoric,* edited by Michelle Ballif, Southern Illinois UP, 2013, pp. 139–53.

Caswell, Michelle, et al. "'To Suddenly Discover Yourself Existing': Uncovering the Impact of Community Archives." *The American Archivist,* vol. 79, no. 1, 2016, pp. 56–81.

Enoch, Jessica, and Pamela VanHaitsma. "Archival Literacy: Reading the Rhetoric of Digital Archives in the Undergraduate Classroom." *College Composition and Communication,* vol. 67, no. 2, 2015, pp. 216–42.

García, Romeo, and José M. Cortez. "The Trace of a Mark That Scatters: The Anthropoi and the Rhetoric of Decoloniality." *Rhetoric Society Quarterly,* vol. 50, no. 2, 2020, pp. 93–108.

Gonzalez, Norma, et al. *Funds of Knowledge: Theorising Practices in Households, Communities, and Classrooms*. Lawrence Erlbaum, 2005.

Hayden, Wendy. "'Gifts' of the Archives: A Pedagogy for Undergraduate Research." *College Composition and Communication,* vol. 66, no. 3, 2015, pp. 402–26.

Kirsch, Gesa E., et al., eds. *Unsettling Archival Research: Engaging Critical Communal, and Digital Archives*. Southern Illinois UP, 2023.

Lyons, Scott Richard. "Rhetorical Sovereignty: What Do American Indians Want from Writing?" *College Composition and Communication*, vol. 51, no. 3, 2000, pp. 447–68.

Martinez, Aja Y. "Core-Coursing Counterstory: On Master Narrative Histories of Rhetorical Studies Curricula." *Rhetoric Review*, vol. 38, no. 4, 2019, pp. 402–16.

Mignolo, Walter. "Delinking." *Cultural Studies*, vol. 21, no. 2–3, 2007, pp. 449–514.

Ndlovu-Gatsheni, Sabelo J. *Epistemic Freedom in Africa: Deprovincialization and Decolonization*. Routledge, 2018.

Powell, Malea. "Listening to Ghosts: An Alternative (Non)Argument." *ALT DIS: Alternative Discourses and the Academy*, edited by Christopher Schroeder, Helen Fox, and Patricia Bizzell, Boynton/Cook-Heinemann, 2002, pp. 139–53.

Purdy, James P. "Three Gifts of Digital Archives." *Journal of Literacy and Technology*, vol. 12, 2011, pp. 24–49.

Ramirez, Loretta. "Archival Quest: Research Writing Pedagogies to Recover Historical Rhetorics That Centralize Latinx Voice and Inquiry." *Composition Studies*, vol. 51, no. 1, 2023, pp. 91–110.

———. "Digging the Archives in Composition Stretch Programs: Reclamation of Historical Rhetorics to Support Chicanx Emotions of Belonging." *College Composition and Communication*, vol. 75, no. 3, forthcoming, 2024.

———. *The Wound and the Stitch: A Genealogy of the Female Body from Medieval Iberia to SoCal Chicanx Art*. Pennsylvania State UP, 2024.

Ruiz, Iris D., and Raúl Sánchez, eds. *Decolonizing Rhetoric and Composition Studies: New Latinx Keywords for Theory and Pedagogy*. Palgrave Macmillan, 2016.

VanHaitsma, Pamela. "New Pedagogical Engagements with Archives: Student Inquiry and Composing in Digital Spaces." *College English*, vol. 78, no. 1, 2015, pp. 34–55.

CHAPTER ELEVEN

An Abundance of Voices: Examining Diverse and International Students' Assumptions about Writing to Cultivate Richer and More Inclusive Writing Classrooms

YASMIN RIOUX
Divine Word College

Writing is a mode of enquiry (Park), an opportunity to grapple with the self, an act of reflection (Pagnucci; Clandinin & Connelly; Clandinin & Huber; Connelly & Clandinin; Bruner, *The Narrative Construction of Reality*; Bruner, *Life as Narrative*), uniquely personal, reflective of cultural impressions and exposures, and much needed as outward mode of communication, especially within higher learning writing classrooms. As assumptions about writing vary based on a writer's/writing student's cultural background, it is imperative that we, as writing instructors, gain a better understanding of what our students associate with the writing process and related items like intellectual property and plagiarism, research practices, and parts of a "standard" essay. To provide students with inclusive, equitable, and culturally respectful writing classrooms, it is therefore imperative that we are aware of the writing-related assumptions our international and multilingual writing students hold when they come to the college classroom because such information allows us to provide them with better instruction and contexts for learning.

In order to better serve our college writing students and for our writing instruction to reflect the context of higher education that is marked by the need to understand, incorporate, and respect diversity, equity, and inclusive pedagogies, I use open-ended questionnaire-based data to explore how my international writing students perceive writing, see academic writing tasks, and explore what general assumptions they make or have about writing practices within and beyond the writing classroom.

Research shows that several of our approaches to teaching are infused with and embedded in colonial, Western ideologies that ignore important truths held by members of other cultures (Reiter) and that inform their assumptions about reality.

These epistemological and ontological divides between mainstream educational practices and our students' perceived realities impact all aspects of life, including education. It is therefore very important to ask our writing students poignant and specific questions regarding their assumptions about elements of the academic reality in order to better understand and, consequently, better serve our students, our own pedagogies, and the higher education context. When we better understand our students, we can serve them more purposefully, successfully, and effectively while empowering them and ourselves (Larke).

Reflecting on our own Eurocentrically informed minds and educational backgrounds that are heavily influenced by colonial practices is an important practice toward more inclusive educational settings that rely on and share ideas of equity and inclusion rather than enforcing limitations, epistemological segregation, and incomplete realities and methodological approaches. By failing to reflect on our assumptions, we risk losing the ability "to change this pattern of reproducing global white supremacy in the classroom" (Steele 56) within our institutional setting and the extended context. Furthermore, by examining our own practices, we can move toward avoiding the detrimental effects of linguistic imperialism (CCCC; Phillipson), which is of high importance, especially given our uniquely diverse student population at my institution.

In a writing classroom, such reflection and critical examination of my own teaching experiences, approaches, and practices is important because the setting allows for a thorough analysis of "White linguistic hegemony" (Baker-Bell 9) that has become, in various places, part of mainstream language and literacy teaching in the US. By understanding my students' literacy practices that affect their classroom writing behaviors, I can (more) effectively strive toward "linguistic justice" (CCCC) and be more culturally responsive in my teaching approaches/pedagogy (CCCC; Larke).

My research focuses on these central questions:

- What assumptions about writing do our writing students have when entering the required undergraduate writing classroom?
- How can we change our practices to better serve our multilingual writers?
- How can we create more equitable and inclusive writing pedagogies that are based on realistic assumptions our multilingual/international students have about writing?
- Echoing Dr. April Baker-Bell's general questions regarding our role as pedagogues in language and literacy education and our students:
  - "How can language and literacy research and teaching work against racial, cultural, and linguistic inequities?
  - What does racial and linguistic justice look like in language and literacy education?" (9).

Study Course and Context

Regarding the student participants' basic demographic information, the students disclosed the following countries as their places of origin or the countries to which they hold a passport: Vietnam, Haiti, Uganda, Mexico, Rwanda, Cameroon, and Kenya; they listed the following languages as their first: Vietnamese, Luganda, Spanish, Creole, French, Kinyarwanda, Limbum, Kikuyu. Some mentioned that they were also fluent in another language such as Limbum, Pidgin English, Kiswahili, English.

Other demographic and contextual aspects were as follows:

- Average participant age: 35
- Average participant time spent in USA: 21.25 mos.

Considering the class from which data for the current study and working paper was gathered, ENG 112 Academic Writing is the second first-year writing course in the institution's mandatory writing sequence. The class teaches student writers to compose research, analysis, and argumentative papers while focusing on critical reading and research skills, academic writing formats and citations, and rhetorical principles. While the current class is reflective of the college in regard to its diverse student body, it is not designed as a composition course for multilingual students.

The prerequired course, ENG 111 Expository Writing, focuses on expository essays, patterns of college essays and writing, organization, style, as well as syntax. The two courses are designed to build on each other and follow a logical sequence in terms of assessment, assignments, and contents.

Methodology and Tool

To address my research questions, I employ an open-ended questionnaire that aims at eliciting information from my student writers, who are the participants for my ongoing study (see the Appendix). I ask students to complete the given questionnaire within the first weeks of the semester in order to gain insights into their assumptions about writing prior to them being exposed to my teachings, which are inevitably influenced by the US context.

Preliminary Findings

As the current working paper is the first part of a larger ongoing research project, the *n* for this initial data collection was rather low. Despite this, the data revealed interesting insights regarding the students' assumptions about writing.

When asked about who the student writers associate with "writers," some mentioned "Musicians," "Monica Arac de Nyeko, best known for writing short stories, essays, poems," "Students, journalists, human sciences professionals," and "teachers and journalists." Regarding the questions of what genres are common in their home country, some student writers explained "music," "Frictions [sic fiction]," "journalism, novels (drama, romantic), investigation," and "Poetry, Story, Comedy, Drama, and Novel: some are fiction, and some are nonfiction." Another student mentioned "three types of Vietnamese literature: oral traditional literature, Chinese–Vietnamese literature, and modern literature or the romanticized alphabets."

When asked about how students see themselves as writers or what writerly characteristics they'd like to improve, students often expressed interest in or challenges with creativity. Here, many answered that they view themselves as "creative" writers, or "I would like to be more creative." One student also mentioned that "creativity" was one thing that made a piece of writing "good."

When asked about common reasons for writing, students explained that writing can be an outward mode of communication to connect with others as they stated that the purpose of writing is to "share or deliver messages," "inform or educate others," "[complete] academic works," "educate the mass and transmit knowledge," and "[inform] the mass and educating [illegible word]." Others found that the primary purpose for why people choose to write was more personal. Some described that people write "to express their experiences," for "keeping memory of events," and for "self-expression." One student mentioned that writing most commonly takes place for "recreation."

Regarding the question of "What is 'good' writing?", most students alluded to or explained the significance of structure and cohesion. The students mentioned that "a clear and structured paper is always appreciated" and that "unity" leads to a qualitatively good piece of writing. Further, "[...] the way I organize my ideas on the paper. Meaning the writings need to have an introduction, body and the conclusion," was understood to make writing "good."

Concerning my research questions (see above), my work hints at potential ideas about how to improve our practices for multilingual writers and how to create more equitable and inclusive writing pedagogies. In the case of my study, a first step might be acknowledging that some writers might assume that writing is generally more associated with creativity, recreation, or occurs primarily for personal endeavors. It seems that students seek to emulate the common writing genres they find in their setting, which, in the current case, focus on being creative. Here, we might decide to emphasize teaching generic components of US academic writing requirements in order to address commonalities and differences between these. By understanding what writing genres are common according to our student writers, we can tailor our assignments and assessments accordingly, and thereby more successfully address our own assumptions about our students' awareness of certain generic requirements that are deeply engrained in our own local cultures and idea(l)s (Rioux).

Per one of my student writer's responses to the question of "Who is your imaginary audience when you write a college essay?", students might surprise us when they envision "our ancestors" instead of who we might assume they are writing to (peers, instructors, etc.). Broadening our own understanding of personal writing assumptions to allow for unexpected answers and scenarios to take place might be one step toward building more inclusive spaces for the teaching of literacy and/or writing; then we can also move toward addressing Baker-Bell's question regarding the role of language and literacy teaching in "racial, cultural, and linguistic inequities" (9).

Further, our writing places can also work against inequities by providing student writers with spaces where they can explore their writer identities freely and openly in an environment where their backgrounds and prior knowledge are respected and viewed as enriching and integral to the academic setting and writing context. Then, "racial and linguistic justice" (Baker-Bell 9) can be formed through dialogic, mutually engaged, multifaceted, and collaborative spaces where assessments, assignments, rubrics, and overall courses are designed with a realistic picture of what our diverse, international, and multilingual students assume when they think about writing and engage in the writing process.

Overall, the student participants clearly viewed themselves as writers with specific characteristics and identified challenges about their writing abilities. They viewed writing as a personal, social, and academic activity that was oftentimes associated with entertainment or recreation, and that they were engaged with in one way or another within and beyond the academic writing classroom.

Limitations

The current sample size was rather small, and more data is needed. Also, as the sample population has completed their first writing course, I would like to carry out my data collection earlier in the students' academic writing career. Lastly, I am interested in distributing the same questionnaire to students who do not identify as multilingual or international to compare answers from both student writer groups.

Overall, it remains clear that if we more effectively understand how our multilingual and international students view themselves as writers, we can more effectively serve them and address their specific needs.

Works Cited

Baker-Bell, April. "'We Been Knowin': Toward an Antiracist Language & Literacy Education." *Journal of Language and Literacy Education*, vol. 16, no. 1, Mar. 2020. EBSCOhost, search.ebscohost.com/login.aspx?direct=true&db=eric&AN=EJ1253929&site=ehost-live.

Bruner, Jerome. "The Narrative Construction of Reality." *Critical Inquiry*, Sept. 1991, pp. 1–21. EBSCOhost, search.ebscohost.com/login.aspx?direct=true&db=pif&AN=PHL1227233&site=ehost-live.

———. "Life as Narrative." *Social Research*, vol. 71, no. 3, 2004, pp. 691–710.

Clandinin, Jean D., and Michael F. Connelly. *Narrative Inquiry*. Jossey-Bass, 2000.

Clandinin, Jean D., and Janice Huber. "Narrative Inquiry: Toward Understanding Life's Artistry." *Curriculum Inquiry*, vol. 32, no. 2, Summer 2002, p. 161. EBSCOhost, https://doi.org/10.1111/1467-873X.00220.

Conference on College Composition and Communication. CCCC Statement on *White Language Supremacy*. 2021, https://cccc.ncte.org/cccc/white-language-supremacy.

Connelly, Michael F., and Jean D. Clandinin. "Stories of Experience and Narrative Inquiry." *Educational Researcher*, vol. 19, no. 5, June 1990, pp. 2–14. EBSCOhost, search.ebscohost.com/login.aspx?direct=true&db=eric&AN=EJ414358&site=ehost-live.

Larke, Patricia. "Culturally Responsive Teaching in Higher Education: What Professors Need to Know." *Counterpoints*, vol. 391, 2013, pp. 38–50. JSTOR, http://www.jstor.org/stable/42981435. Accessed 17 Jan. 2024.

Pagnucci, Gian. *Living the Narrative Life*. Boynton/Cook, 2004.

Park, Gloria. "'Writing Is a Way of Knowing': Writing and Identity." *ELT Journal: English Language Teaching Journal*, vol. 67, no. 3, July 2013, pp. 336–45. EBSCOhost, https://doi.org/10.1093/elt/cct012.

Phillipson, Robert. *Linguistic Imperialism*. Oxford University Press, 1992.

Reiter, Bernd. "Fuzzy Epistemology: Decolonizing the Social Sciences." *Journal for the Theory of Social Behaviour*, vol. 50, no. 1, Mar. 2020, pp. 103–18. EBSCOhost, https://doi.org/10.1111/jtsb.12229.

Rioux, Yasmin. "New Encounters with an Old Course: Rethinking My Composition Course Approaches for a Highly Diverse Class." *College English Association Forum*, vol. 49, no. 2, 2023, pp. 216–27.

Steele, Chris. "Decolonizing the Classroom: Embracing Radical Internationalism." *Radical Teacher*, no. 110, Winter 2018, pp. 55–57. EBSCOhost, https://doi.org/10.5195/rt.2018.441.

University of North Carolina at Chapel Hill Writing Center. "Writing Inventory." 2023. https://writingcenter.unc.edu/tips-and-tools/writing-groups/writing-group-starter-kit/writing-inventory/.

Appendix: Questionnaire (condensed)

When answering the given questions, please reflect on your current knowledge and understanding and use the cultural identity that you feel most comfortable with as a reference point. If you cannot answer a question, simply skip it!

Demographics:

Please:

- Provide your age:
- List the country for which you hold a passport:
- List your first language:
- List any additional languages you consider yourself fluent in:
- List how many months/years you've lived in the USA:
- List the English classes in which you are currently enrolled:

General Questions about writing in your home culture:

Reflecting on the culture that you identify with the most:

1. Who writes frequently?
2. Why do people write? What is their purpose or objective for/when writing?
3. What are some very common genres of writing in your home country?
4. What thoughts or information goes into your own writing?
5. What is good writing? What makes a piece of writing "good"?
6. What is plagiarism? How do individuals avoid it or contribute to it?
7. What can you include as evidence in a formal (academic) paper?
8. What is acceptable evidence for research in an academic setting?
9. What do you choose to include in a narrative when you are asked to write one? What do you choose to omit? Why?
10. Who is your imaginary audience when you write a college essay? Who do you picture?
11. Where do you find knowledge for research?
12. Who has knowledge? Who, if anyone, does knowledge belong to?
13. Can anyone "own" knowledge/information?

Writing Specific:

1. What, if any, is the relationship between reading and writing?

2. What is a thesis statement in an essay/paper? What does it do for your writing and audience? What is its purpose?

3. What is a topic sentence and what does it do for your writing and audience? What is its purpose?

4. What is the purpose of an introduction?

5. What is the purpose of a conclusion?

You, the Student Writer—writerly, culturally embedded identity (adapted from University of North Carolina at Chapel Hill Writing Center. "Writing Inventory" https://writingcenter.unc.edu/tips-and-tools/writing-groups/writing-group-starter-kit/writing-inventory/.):

Please reflect on your first language AND English.

1. What is your personal favorite kind of writing and why?

2. What type of writing do you engage with regularly? (Incl. social media, letters, emails, poems, etc.)

3. What is your favorite part about writing? What are some things you are particularly good at?

4. What do you find most challenging as a writer?

5. Please use 3 adjectives to describe yourself as a writer.

6. If you had the ability to change one thing about your writing, what would it be?

CHAPTER TWELVE

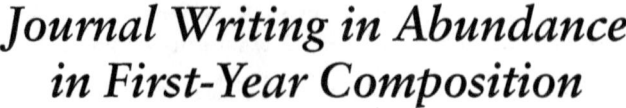

Journal Writing in Abundance in First-Year Composition

Kylie Skeel
Tiffin University

Introduction

Twenty-five percent of first-time first-year bachelor's degree seeking students will drop out of college after their first year (Hanson). Those students are also more likely to be BIPOC students due to the systemic racism that often characterizes higher education institutions. However, first-year composition is the perfect place to build a student's confidence in order to increase retention amongst students and help them in achieving success. Journal writing is an honest and inclusive way to engage students in first-year composition to become more acclimated to appreciating the writing process and mitigating the feeling of giving up on their college careers, especially for BIPOC students. When students first get to college, everything is new and uncomfortable. Finding a genre that is low-stakes and helps them be comfortable is key to building confidence in the writing process for first-year composition students.

After receiving IRB approval at my university, I piloted a study in my first-year composition classroom to find out if journal writing was actually helping BIPOC students in my classroom evolve their writing skills. I chose BIPOC students because my dissertation was centered around Black women first-generation college students, and I know first-hand that the research says that BIPOC students face more barriers in the first-year composition classroom (Skeel 2023). However, I decided to add a layer to their journal writing for the semester: Wardle's theory of writing about writing. While writing about writing can sometimes be a controversial topic and focus because first-year students do not have a full grasp on the realm of writing studies quite yet, I wondered if employing this theory into low-stakes journal writing would assist BIPOC students in becoming more comfortable in the first-year composition classroom. Journal writing in abundance is an assignment that I have always required in the first-year composition classroom because many students would tell me it was like therapy to have dedicated quiet time to themselves each week to just write and explore their writing. However, adding Wardle's theory of writing about writing would put a different twist on the journal writing in the classroom, and my hope was that students could discover their strengths and weaknesses within their own writing.

Methods

My methods within this study centered writing, ethics, and feminism. To start, I employed Wardle's theory (found in *Writing About Writing*) within the journal writing genre. I also utilized Mortensen and Kirsch's *Ethics and Representation in Qualitative Studies of Literacy*, where they explain that those in the field of rhetoric and writing must be aware of the various moral and ethical standards that we must uphold as researchers who are conducting qualitative data. Keeping their work in mind, I wanted to ensure that I am being the most ethical and moral researcher possible within my work by keeping in mind that I will never understand what it is like to be a BIPOC student in higher education. I also wanted to ensure that I was getting truth and honesty from my participant and that my position as a white woman faculty member did not influence the participant's answers. Therefore, instead of traditional interviews, I opted to provoke the student with questions via Google Docs. She then had three weeks to return answers to me. This student was not only involved in athletics, but she was also working a part-time job and going to school full-time. Therefore, I wanted to accommodate her schedule because I truly appreciated her willingness to participate and share her experiences. Also, when I analyzed the data in Excel and utilized inductive coding, I had to keep in mind that as a white faculty member, I was automatically in a position of power; I needed to ensure that the data let the student's words tell the story and that I, as the researcher, was merely the presenter of the story. Lastly, due to interviewing a Black woman participant in this study, I also kept in mind Cheryl Glenn's *Rhetorical Feminism and This Thing Called Hope*. Glenn explains,

> Rhetorical feminism offers us a productive tactic for reflecting on and generating histories as well. Scholars can start by disidentifying with hegemonic rhetorical histories, thinking creatively and strategically, engaging in dialogues with traditional and feminist scholars alike, and listening to the vernaculars, emotions, and experiences of rhetors who reside at the margins—all in an attempt to understand other points of view and research stances, all toward the goal of expanding and enriching our rhetorical histories. (113)

Therefore, in the spirit of journaling, I kept my own reflective journal throughout this study and took notes on how I can also be a better feminist, especially for BIPOC women, in my first-year composition classroom.

Participation and Context

In fall 2023, I marketed my study to my students in first-year composition. I ended up having one participant, who identified as a Black woman. I gave her a set of one round of interview questions to answer via Google Docs in the first few weeks of the semester and then gave her another set of interview questions right before finals week. I purposely let her answer the questions via Google Docs rather than in a formal interview since the heart of this study was centered around freewriting and journal writing. I wanted it to be a very low-stakes environment and one where she could write anything she wanted without the fear of judgment or trying to answer the questions tailored around what I was looking for. I wanted her to answer them openly and honestly. Below are the assignment instructions for journal writing in my first-year composition class.

Journal Entries: The only way to get better at writing is to keep doing it! Journal entries serve as an informal way of making writing a habit. You can write about literally anything you want, but I will provide a topic weekly for those who need some guidance. Every week you will get 20–30 minutes of quiet time in class to write in your journal. I suggest you keep your journal on Google Docs and title your entries depending on the week/date to keep track. You will have 10 entries total and each entry should be in Times New Roman font, size 12, double-spaced, and a minimum of one page. When you submit your journal in week 10, it should minimally be <u>10 pages double-spaced with 10 entries</u>. Grading for the journal entries will be based on meeting minimal requirements. Due to journal entries sometimes becoming personal or emotional, I do not give feedback. The journals should be used for you to freewrite and be creative. You will receive full credit as long as it is 10 pages double-spaced total and there is an entry for each week when submitted. Below you will find optional topics for each week:

- <u>Week One</u>: What is the hardest element about writing for you and why?
- <u>Week Two</u>: What is the easiest element about writing for you and why?
- <u>Week Three</u>: What is your history and relationship with writing?
- <u>Week Four</u>: What type of writing is your favorite and why?
- <u>Week Five</u>: How do you use writing in your life right now?
- <u>Week Six</u>: How will you use writing in your future job someday?
- <u>Week Seven</u>: Now that we are at the halfway point in the semester, have your feelings about writing changed? Why or why not?
- <u>Week Eight</u>: How has your writing evolved over the years?
- <u>Week Nine</u>: Use this week's journal to vent about anything you want.
- <u>Week Ten</u>: Now that you have spent the bulk of the semester writing about writing in your journals, how has it changed you as a writer or has it not? Have you ever had to write about writing? Was it weird? How has your writing changed just in this class?

You cannot use AI for this assignment.

As one can see, the main focus within the journal writing assignment was writing about writing, which was different than what I typically do because normally I prompt questions that are personal and allow me to get to know my students on a deeper level. I also stated that I did not want AI to be used in this assignment because journal writing in abundance is supposed to be personal and an avenue for students to get to know their own writing strengths and weaknesses better. While my employer has taken a very open access approach to AI, I feel that this is one of those assignments where it does not make sense to utilize AI as a tool.

Findings

Throughout this small study, I found that Wardle's writing-about-writing theory within journal writing was helpful for this specific BIPOC student in this study. While there are some elements I would change, I want to focus on the positive aspects that came out of this study. The student I interviewed stated that the journal prompts and journaling in general helped to change her mind about writing. She said in high school she constantly felt like she needed to code-switch and, ultimately, had a very negative mindset around writing. However, coming to college and getting in the habit of journaling in first-year composition allowed her to see writing in a different way. She now looked at writing as though it can be low stakes, it can be low pressure, and it can be a way to discover your own writing strengths. The participant stated, "I feel like the more I write, the more it helps me with the way I voice myself in many situations" (2023). Therefore, journaling also allowed her to find her voice not only in first-year composition but also in everyday rhetorical situations.

    The participant in this study also stated that she felt having time to herself in class to dedicate to make her writing better made her feel more confident as well. She said that she never took an English class where she was "forced" to think about what aspects of her writing are "good" and what aspects of her writing needed to grow. She said she was just in the high school habit of reading something, writing about it, and having a teacher who marked her paper up in red pen or put so many comment bubbles on the paper that it was overwhelming. She said she liked that in my feedback on her formal papers I would always start with a point of praise and then give her feedback that would help her writing evolve. But she also said that the journal prompts allowed her to think about her writing more in a rhetorical way rather than just being more "robotic" about her writing process: reading, writing, and receiving criticism. She now viewed the writing process as a whole differently and *positively* and said that now before she starts a major writing assignment, she journals about the assignment before starting her outline to get a better idea of how she wants to tackle a major paper in any given class. All of these elements surfacing in our interview questions really made me feel a lot better about the way I teach first-year composition and allow me to see that I teach first-year composition in an inclusive way.

Conclusion

As first-year composition instructors, we need to keep student success and comfort at the forefront of our classrooms, especially for BIPOC students because they need to feel supported and they need to be retained in order for them to obtain their degrees. Too often BIPOC students drop out due to lack of resources. As FYC teachers, let's be that support that they need and help them achieve their goals. In this study, journaling allowed the student to have a safe environment to explore her own strengths and weaknesses within her writing skills without the pressure of her peers or me. It also allowed her to reflect on why she initially did not like writing in high school and why her feelings have since changed. Journaling about her writing and making writing studies the sole focus of the journals in our class allowed the participant to have a safe space for her writing, and this result is really what we should strive for with our students. BIPOC students encounter way more barriers in the first-year composition classroom than their white peers. Writing teachers need to consider adding a journal writing component to allow BIPOC students to be comfortable and find their voice in the writing classroom and evolve their personal writing skills in a low-stakes way.

Works Cited

Glenn, Cheryl. *Rhetorical Feminism and This Thing Called Hope.* Southern Illinois UP, 2018. EBSCOhost, search.ebscohost.com/login.aspx?direct=true&db=e000xna&AN=1905143&site=eds-live&scope=site.

Hanson, Melanie. "College Dropout Rates." *Education Data Initiative,* 29 Oct. 2023, educationdata.org/college-dropout-rates#:~:text=First%2Dtime%20undergraduate%20first%2Dyear,up%20to%2040%25%20drop%20out. Accessed 18 Jan. 2024.

Mortensen, Peter, and Gesa Kirsch, editors. *Ethics and Representation in Qualitative Studies of Literacy.* NCTE, 1996.

Skeel, Kylie. *"We Should All Be Feminists": Supporting Black Women First-Generation College Students in the Writing Classroom.* 2023. Bowling Green State University, Doctoral dissertation. OhioLINK Electronic Theses and Dissertations Center, http://rave.ohiolink.edu/etdc/view?acc_num=bgsu167957247764171.

Wardle, Elizabeth. *Writing about Writing.* 4th ed., Bedford/St. Martin's, 2020. EBSCOhost, search.ebscohost.com/login.aspx?direct=true&db=cat02507a&AN=ohiolink.b42049382&site=eds-live&scope=site.

CHAPTER THIRTEEN

A View from the ALPs: Teaching-Track Faculty and the Digital Pedagogical Mentorship of Graduate Student Instructors in the Active-Learning Pods Model

GABRIELLE STECHER
Indiana University Bloomington

As Associate Director of Undergraduate Teaching in the English Department at Indiana University Bloomington, one of my core beliefs is that graduate students have a right to an abundance of pedagogical mentorship. Pedagogical mentorship and teaching-related professional development should not be limited to a single semester teaching practicum at the beginning of their graduate program and any subsequent voluntary or ad-hoc participation in professional development. "Jumbo" composition courses, serving nearly one hundred students, certainly possess their share of logistical and pedagogical challenges. Yet, these courses can create important opportunities for meaningful and persistent mentorship, particularly where digital pedagogy is concerned.

In this brief essay, I showcase my approach to mentoring graduate student instructors serving as "co-teachers" in my large, digital projects-based composition course at IUB. A newly launched course, ENG-W171 fulfills the freshman composition requirement at IUB. Each semester, a faculty member leads a large, 96-student section with three embedded graduate student co-teachers; these sections are intended as opportunities to train and advise new instructors who, we hope, will eventually spin off to lead their own smaller and self-designed sections of the digital projects course. Through this experience, graduate students practice not only classroom management skills and active learning strategies in an unfamiliar learning environment; for most, this is their introduction to digital pedagogy and how to design courses with an explicit focus on digital literacy and creativity. Ultimately, I argue that these courses, when developed and led by non-tenure-track faculty, are unique opportunities to provide crucial mentoring to graduate students outside of spaces, such as exam or dissertation committees, that NTT faculty traditionally lack access to. Mentoring graduate student instructors in this environment makes NTT service and pedagogical labor all the more visible while also ensuring that graduate students receive strategic guidance on leveraging digital tools in their classrooms and beyond. This is not to say that the burden of pedagogical mentorship can or should be placed on NTT faculty; to prevent burnout and not exploit the labor and enthusiasm of instructional faculty, this is not a model that should be repeatedly taught by the same NTT faculty member each semester. Rather, I suggest that this model, when supported by several NTT faculty who willingly rotate into this position, can simultaneously serve graduate students while spotlighting NTT expertise in teaching and learning, further making visible their intellectual contributions and service to the department or writing program.

Contextualizing the Active Learning Pods Model

While "jumbo" composition courses are not new, the IUB English ALPs model puts a digital spin on large-enrollment writing courses. As Kim Jaxon, Laura Sparks, and Chris Fosen have articulated, "jumbo" courses (following the California State University, Chico, model) allow for the distribution of expertise between the instructor and the course's student writing mentors (117). Further, "the jumbo is an intentional and student-centered innovation that leverages the institutional environment and students' and faculty's expertise, with student participation and professional development for future teachers as core principles" (117). But what happens when the model is reimagined explicitly for the professionalization of graduate students in the middle of their teaching contract who have some experience teaching the department's standard composition curriculum but would like to learn more about the art of course design and digital pedagogy?

In 2021, Miranda Rodak, Director of Undergraduate Teaching, successfully proposed the creation of ENG-W171, and with it came her vision of the ALPs, or active-learning pods, a model that marries graduate student pedagogical training with a dynamic undergraduate learning experience. The ALPs model brings ninety-six students, three graduate student co-instructors, and a faculty lead/curriculum designer into an active learning classroom that has been carefully constructed by IU's Mosaic Initiative. Through leveraging learning spaces that privilege high-impact pedagogical practices and educational technology, ALPs sections become active learning, digital laboratories where students experiment in a team-based setting while graduate students serve as guides and interact with faculty in real time as they design and lead a digital composition course. The course was first piloted in the fall of 2022 by Justin Hodgson, whose Minecraft class, in partnership with UITS [University Information Technology Services] Learning Technologies and the IU Archives, invites students to explore a range of digital writing practices using the IU Bloomington campus as their grounding artifact. Students recreate key campus structures, buildings, and spaces in Minecraft EDU and design immersive experiences for visitors to our Minecraft EDU world(s). Each of the structures built in Minecraft EDU includes layers of in-game content (embedded and/or linked to external web locations) related to student work throughout the semester: from personal connections to historical significance, from scrolling digital essays to playable audio/visual media (Rodak & Hodgson).

Though I am continually in awe of Hodgson's innovative pedagogy, my approach to developing ENG-W171 curriculum abandons the video game element and instead solely embraces select applications from the Adobe Creative Cloud. As an inquiry-driven course inspired by my scholarship on women artist narratives, my students interrogate through a series of multimodal projects the mediated afterlives of Marilyn Monroe and her enigmatic presence in American popular culture. Throughout the semester, students harness the creative potential of three Adobe tools, increasing in complexity, to tell their own stories about the star and the contexts in which she worked. Balancing topical inquiry with digital skills and products is a conversation for another day; my focus here is on how I mentor graduate students to harness these tools for their own professional development.

Digital Creativity, Pedagogy, and Empowerment of Graduate Student Instructors

When I was tapped to lead an ALPs section for the first time in fall 2023, I began to envision an experience in which both undergraduates and graduate students alike would walk away from the semester feeling creatively empowered. Aside from ensuring that my course aligned with our program's standardized outcomes, I wanted, above all else, for my graduate student co-instructors to not feel dismissed as graders and on-the-ground tech support and instead feel empowered to exercise their creativity in the classroom. Three core values underlie my ENG-W171 curriculum: curiosity, creativity, and collaboration, and they apply as much to the undergraduates as the graduate students.

Putting to the side the digital piece that differentiates ENG-W171 from the standardized version of composition that all graduate students teach when they enter the program, the ALPs model is often the first time that the art of intentional course design is made transparent to early- to mid-career graduate student instructors who have been teaching standardized curricula prior to this experience. A healthy curiosity about the mechanics of intentional course design and the ability to dissect our course's scaffold leads to more generative brainstorming when it comes time for the graduate students to begin the process of proposing their own course after the semester they are embedded in the ALPs model. But curiosity also extends to experimenting with new digital tools. Graduate students in the literature track who possess a more "traditional" mindset about what scholarship and pedagogy should look like tend to be more hesitant about educational technology and the ways that digital tools can transform our scholarship for the better. In some ways, I feel that I am especially equipped to mentor these graduate students as I am a Victorianist by training who has shifted by desire and necessity into new digital scholarly and pedagogical spaces. In any case, the ALPs model is often the first time that these graduate students have been encouraged to experiment with digital tools to produce multimodal scholarship and curricular artifacts. I discuss how I mentor graduate students to use these tools on their own below. But in order to create alignment between our course values, the curriculum and student learning outcomes, and the methods of delivery, I create a collaborative digital space in which we can map out these mechanics. Trello, a team-based project management tool, allows us to create and manipulate curriculum map using a series of cards and lists organized by unit. Such a visual tool (in combination with my Digital Skills Crescendo, which I have shared as an open educational resource) demystifies course design and allows the instructional team to spot moments in each unit plan where we can work individually and collaboratively to create new multimodal resources (Stecher). After all, if ENG-W171 is all about making digital tools like Trello and the Adobe Creative Cloud work for me, my co-instructors, and our students, it begins with a strong grasp of course design.

On Teaching the Art of Self-Promotion with Digital Tools

As an early-career administrator and teaching faculty, I have quickly learned the importance and value of self-promotion. Leaning into digital pedagogy, and by extension digital creativity, has revolutionized my process for developing curricular assets that do double duty: they provide engaging resources for my students while serving as documentation of teaching innovation that I can promote across various platforms, ranging from my promotion dossier to my personal website and online teaching portfolio. The ability to use and leverage the unique affordances of digital tools such as Adobe Creative Cloud and Canva to make transparent my pedagogical labor and expertise in course design while promoting my scholarship is something I wish I had learned sooner. As such, I make it a point to consistently encourage my co-instructors to use the very digital skills and tools exercised in ENG-W171 for their own academic self-promotion. It does not matter how early in the graduate program a co-instructor is. It is never too early to be proactive and provide them with the concrete tools and strategies they will need to succeed on the changing job market, regardless of the path (academic or industry) they choose.

Whenever co-instructors create curricular assets for our course, I ask them to use the same tools assigned in class so that students can see how we each model our own use of them for professional purposes. The co-instructors, for example, use Adobe Express to create infographics that remediate content from textbook readings or capture highlights from in-class discussions. I emphasize that these assets do not have to live and die in this course, left forgotten in a folder on the cloud to never be reopened. Being strategic about the creation of curricular assets means (1) leveraging the technology (such as the industry standard but prohibitively expensive for individual users Adobe Creative Cloud) that they have access to while students at IUB and (2) creating materials that can be disseminated as open educational resources and via their own portfolio website. The end of the semester tasks students with creating a portfolio website that serves as a reflective record of learning. As we teach students best practices for developing an authentic personal brand and narrativizing the purpose and production contexts of their creations, I similarly encourage the graduate students to simultaneously begin developing and promoting their own unique brand identities as teacher-scholars. Regardless of the student's identity or positionality, I understand my role to be a mentor who can help democratize access to the strategies and tools they can leverage to more intentionally promote themselves and their work in digital spaces as they prepare for the job market and other creative endeavors. Developing a portfolio website is an iterative process that requires a great time (and sometimes financial) investment; however, this is labor worth undertaking, and the sooner they begin this work, the better. I am candid about my own portfolio creation process, and I refuse to gatekeep what I have learned.

As a literature-trained, teaching-track faculty member and administrator, I recognize all too well the tensions that exist in the academic and professional trajectories of English graduate students. In departments where traditional literary scholarship reigns supreme, expertise in pedagogy, much less digital pedagogy, can be brushed aside as an "extracurricular," or a less-than-necessary investment of one's time and intellectual labor. The pedagogical mentorship of research-first advisory committees only extends so far, and unless the graduate student is on a digital humanities or rhetoric track, we cannot expect that they will receive up-to-date, much less strategic guidance on digital pedagogy and, with it, scholarship of teaching and learning. My position as an early-career faculty member with recent job market experience has inspired me to take seriously any opportunity to empower graduate students in digital spaces, and the ALPs model is a landmark in my journey toward a wholehearted investment in the professional development of English graduate students.

Works Cited

Jaxon, Kim, et al. "Epic Learning in a 'Jumbo' Writing Course." *Composition Studies*, vol. 48, no. 2, 2020, p. 116–27.

Rodak, Miranda, and Justin Hodgson. Interview by Sarah Engel. *The Connected Professor,* Spring 2023, https://connectedprof.iu.edu/articles/2023-spring/more-active-more-digital-more-impactful.html. Accessed January 27, 2024.

Stecher, Gabrielle. "Digital Skills Crescendo." Humanities Commons CORE Repository, August 2023, https://hcommons.org/deposits/item/hc:58057.

CHAPTER FOURTEEN

Black Community Colleges: A History and Appraisal

HOWARD TINBERG
Bristol Community College

I. The Other Historically Black Colleges

For several years now, prominent scholars of composition have called for a more expansive history of our discipline, with special attention to be paid to marginalized institutions and to the faculty and students who labor within (Royster and Williams; Gilyard; Gold; Zaluda; Moss; Jarrett; Jackson et al.). Heeding that call, I attempt in this essay to add to our discipline's reach by focusing on the history of Historically Black Community Colleges (HBCCs), "a seldom-discussed and -studied category of institutions" (Elliott et al. 770). That history will show that HBCCs have played a pioneering role not only in providing access to higher education for students of color and the opportunities that resulted from such access, but they have also been at the forefront of promoting the values of equity, inclusion, and social justice.

HBCCs make up about 12% of all Historically Black Colleges and Universities (Gassman; "On Their Own Terms" 6). They enroll roughly 50,000 students each year (Strayhorn) and award on average 3,800 associate degrees (Gassman). Nationally, they serve 3% of students who attend college, with a much larger percentage in the South, where most of the HBCCs are located (Gassman; "On Their Own Terms" 6).

Currently, enrollment at two-year HBCCs consists of 81% Black students and 10% white students ("On Their Own Terms"). Eighty-five percent attend full-time, in contrast with 21% full-time Black students at non-Minority Serving Institutions (MSIs) ("On Their Own Terms").

The economic impact of HBCUs has been well documented. A study commissioned by the United Negro College Fund (UNCF) in 2014 estimates, for example, that HBCUs generate $14.8 billion annually in spending, over 134,000 jobs, and $130 billion in lifetime earnings for their graduates ("HBCU's Make America Strong" 5). A Gallup Poll from 2014–15 affirmed that Black HBCU grads were more likely to achieve well-being—financial, social, community, and physical well-being—than Black graduates of non-HBCUs (Seymour and Ray).

Historically Black Community Colleges play an important role in providing access to higher education and thus serve as an impetus for such economic gains. The years between 1995 and 2015 saw enrollment growth at HBCCs for Black, Hispanic and Latinx, and American Indian and Alaskan native students (Elliott et al. 779). In that same span, the number of Pell Grant recipients at HBCCs increased by 25% (Elliott et al. 779). A study done by Thomas Bailey and colleagues in 2006 that used as a measure of success a comparison of graduation and transfer rates at community colleges showed that "the performance of historically black community colleges is roughly 13 percent higher than other institutions" (Bailey et al. 24).

In constructing the history of Black community colleges, two caveats need to be offered. First, many Historically Black Universities (HBUs) did not begin their existence as full-fledged universities but rather had more modest beginnings, for example as normal schools for teacher education or vocational training sites for freed slaves or, in fact, precollegiate institutions aimed at providing Blacks with essential literacies. Their mission was quite similar to that of the modern community college, with a historical focus on basic and generalizable skills. Cheyney University, often cited as the first HBU, is a case in point. Begun in 1837, Cheyney, then known as Cheyney College, the Institute for Colored Youth, was founded by a Quaker philanthropist as the Institute for Colored Youth in Cheyney, Pennsylvania, with the core purpose of fostering freed slaves' skills in reading, writing, and math (Lovitt, 12; Edmondson).

Second, the terms used to distinguish the Historically Black Two-Year College from its four-year counterpart were not always available early in its history. The term *community college,* of course, is a relatively recent coinage, entering common usage with the Report of the Truman Commission of 1947 (Galizio and Boggs). Earlier, the term *junior college* started to have some salience with the founding of non-HBCU Joliet Junior College in 1901, at the urging of William Rainey Harper, president of the University of Chicago (Galizio and Boggs). Yet even that term has limited utility when tracing the origin of HBCCs, where early "junior colleges" are designated with terms such as "Mississippi Southern Christian Institute" (founded 1895) or "Morristown Normal and Industrial College," begun in 1910 (Lane 277). Instead of relying on these terms as designators, I will instead highlight key aspects of the missions of these pioneering HBCCs that recall the function, values, and priorities of the modern, two-year college.

Historically Black Community Colleges, like many colleges that would become four-year institutions, came into existence through the efforts of religious groups such as the African Methodist Episcopal Church and the American Baptist Home Mission Societies (Elliott et al. 771). These groups advocated for the principle of education for all.

II. The First Historically Black Community Colleges

The "Directory of Junior Colleges, 1933," published in the *Junior College Journal,* lists some 21 colleges for Blacks, with most located in Texas (Lane 273). The Directory gives these as among the earliest:

- 1895 Southern Christian Institute (Mississippi)
- 1910 Morristown Normal and Industrial College (Tennessee)
- 1912 Normal and Agricultural College (Georgia)
- 1918 Oakwood College (Alabama)
- 1920 State A. & M. College for Negroes (Alabama)

- 1921 Storer College (West Virginia)
- 1923 Bethune-Cookman College (Florida)
- 1925 Princess Anne Academy (Maryland)
  - Brick Junior College (North Carolina)
  - Mary Allen Seminary (Texas)
- 1926 Jarvis Christian College (Texas)

(Lane 276)

Identifying the first "Historically Black Community College" is difficult in part because of the problem of terminology mentioned above but also because of the narrow mission of some of these early colleges, whether it be to train students to spread the gospel or to serve exclusively as a school for teachers only. One scholar offers this speculation and analysis of possible contenders for the first HBCC:

> Oakwood College, to which the date 1918 is assigned, should probably not be looked upon as a "pure" junior college, since its avowed purpose is "to supply the twelve million colored people of this country with gospel workers" and since its catalogue shows it to be essentially a theological and Bible-training institution. In the opinion of the writer, based upon the materials of this study, Walden College, Nashville, Tennessee, although it is now extinct, may lay claim to having been the first "pure" junior college for Negroes. The report of the 1928 federal survey of Negro colleges and universities stated: "Since its reopening in 1919 Walden College has been organized on a junior college basis, two-year curricula being offered in arts, in science or premedical work, in education, and in home economics. A high school and an elementary school are also conducted. . . . The graduates of Walden College have been accepted with full junior standing at Northwestern University, Ohio University, and Clark University." (Lane 277)

Noteworthy here are the following aspects of Walden's mission, which mirror the missions of the modern two-year college: allusions to general education ("arts . . . science") as well as practical and job-related training ("home economics") and perhaps vocational skills ("premedical"), in addition to the vital matter of transfer to four-year colleges.

Among HBCCs still operating, Shorter College, a private, two-year college located in North Little Rock, Arkansas, has the clearest claim to being the oldest HBCC in the country, having been founded in 1886 by the African Methodist Episcopal Church ("About Us"; Lovitt 19). While explicitly calling itself a "Christian College," Shorter sees "faith and learning as inextricably linked" and is firmly committed to prepare its students to become curious, productive, and faithful citizens ("About Us"). I will say more about the distinctive mission and curricula of HBCCs, but it's important to note that while Shorter, like so many other two-year colleges, is committed both to general education and job preparation, it also sees itself as a center to transmit and preserve African American heritage and culture ("About Us").

All told, there are twelve HBCCs currently in operation, all located in the Southern states and virtually all public colleges:

- Bishop State Community College, Alabama, est. 1927
- Coahoma Community College, Mississippi, est. 1924
- Denmark Technical College, South Carolina, est. 1948
- Gadsden State Community College, Alabama, est. 1925
- H. Councill Trenholm State Community College, Alabama, est. 1961
- Hinds Community College at Utica, Mississippi, est. 1903
- J. F. Drake State Community and Technical College, Alabama, est. 1962
- Lawson State Community College-Birmingham Campus, Alabama, est. 1949
- Shelton State Community College, Alabama, est. 1952
- Shorter College, Arkansas, est. 1886
- Southern University at Shreveport, Louisiana, est. 1967
- St. Philip's College, Texas, est. 1898

(Elliott et al. 776)

III. The Mission of Historically Black Community Colleges

With the end of the Civil War and the passing of the 13th Amendment, the founding of colleges for African Americans was built on the idea that education was the "ultimate emancipator" (Allen et al.). Education provided freed slaves with the necessary skills to allow them to be truly free—that is, able to enjoy the fruits of genuine citizenship, which included the promise of social mobility. Resistance among Southern whites to the granting of literacy to freed slaves did not deter African Americans and their sponsors from building colleges explicitly designed to endow the formerly enslaved with the skills necessary to prosper as free men and women.

In the early 20th century, as more Black colleges were established, prominent African American educators engaged in a debate about the proper emphasis of Black higher education—a debate that seems so resonant for those of us who teach at the modern two-year college: should the emphasis rest with vocational training or with the liberal arts, or more broadly general education? (Allen et al. 267–68; Early 92). The most prominent advocate for the vocational mission of Black colleges was Booker T. Washington, who saw a practical education as the surest way for Blacks to achieve economic parity with whites. In opposition stood W. E. B. Du Bois, who firmly believed that the best way to achieve parity with whites was for Blacks to enjoy the same classical and humanities-based curriculum that educated whites experienced. Du Bois would go on to argue for a curriculum that also contains elements of Black humanism, the contributions of Black culture to Western society, anticipating the Negro Arts Movement of the 1920s and the demands by Black students in the 1960s and 1970s for a curriculum that reflected Black accomplishments and values (Early 98).

It is worth noting that demands for curricular reform that so dominated the '60s and '70s on college campuses were expressed by students at then Oakwood Junior College decades before. Located in Huntsville, Alabama, Oakwood Junior College was founded by Seventh Day Adventists (SDA) in November 1896 as Oakwood Industrial School, whose mission, directed by an all-white administration, was to give African Americans an "industrial education" with emphasis on "agriculture, carpentry, masonry, domestic service, and horticulture" (Fisher 113–14). A spirit of student activism distinguished the college from its early years. In 1918, Oakwood student Elsie Graves staged a strike to protest against the all-white administration at the college (Fisher 114). More extensive protests occurred in the late '20s and early '30s as students expressed their displeasure over what they perceived as an "overseer plantation relationship" between students and administration (Fisher 114). In 1931, students demanded the appointment of a Black president as well as greater emphasis on the liberal arts (Fisher 114). Protestors were able to achieve the ouster of the white president and the appointment of an African American successor (114).

Like most two-year colleges, HBCCs offer curricula that meet the needs of their communities and the students who live in them, even as they acknowledge their unique origins and missions as Historically Black Colleges. St. Phillips College in San Antonio, Texas, is a good example. Named "One of the Best Community Colleges" in Texas, St. Phillips occupies the important distinction of being a Historically Black College as well as a Hispanic-Serving Institution (HSI) (Morgan). Founded in 1898 by an Episcopalian bishop, St. Phillips began as a private, vocational school for Black girls, became a junior college in 1902, and eventually became affiliated with San Antonio College, joining the public, Alamo Independent School District in 1942 ("Historical Sketch"). A comprehensive, open access college, it remains true to its early vocational mission in promoting workforce and career development even as it stands committed to providing developmental education for those not quite ready to do college-level work, giving a firm foundation in the arts and sciences and preparing students for transfer to a four-year college. Community engagement remains a key component of the college's mission, attending to the needs of a diverse population and thereby creating "an environment of healing and transformation" ("Mission").

IV. Remembering the Brick School and Junior College and the Continuing Mission of Historically Black Community Colleges

To fully appreciate the significant role that Historically Black Community Colleges have had in empowering Black students, we turn, briefly, to the story of a junior college no longer in existence but whose legacy needs to be shared and cherished. In the town of Enfield, just 70 miles northeast of Raleigh, North Carolina, and on the grounds of a former plantation used to "break in" slaves (including the use of a whipping post) and whose slave labor tilled the fertile soil, once stood the Brick School, founded in 1895 by a wealthy donor from Brooklyn, NY, Julia Elmer Brick, who purchased the plantation to foster the education of Black youths ("The Brick School"). She would hand over the plantation grounds to the American Missionary Association, paying for the construction of buildings and the ongoing maintenance of the School. The Brick School, which would become a junior college in 1925, saw its mission as combining both a commitment to the humanities and to vocational training: classroom instruction in the liberal arts was required alongside work demanding manual labor ("The Brick School"). Under its founding principal and head of school, Thomas Sewell Inborden, Brick, which through a work study program was open to all students, assisted in the training of Black farmers in modern framing methods and contributed to the building of a Black professional class in the region. Forced to close in 1933 because of reduction in support from the American Missionary Association and declining enrollment, Brick School and Junior College nonetheless continues to hold a special place of honor in its commitment to promoting "liberty and the larger life" to the Black community ("The Brick School").

Historically Black Community Colleges like the Brick School have indeed served to deliver on the promise of freedom. Providing a powerful template for open access decades before the expansion of community colleges of the 1960s, HBCCs continue to serve underrepresented populations including first generation students of color and the economically disadvantaged. As charter members of Historically Black Colleges and Universities, HBCCs continue to serve as a vital pipeline for minority students to four-year HBUs. Indeed, a recent report issued by the Annenberg Institute at Brown University found that Black students who were enrolled at HBUs were nearly 15% more likely to graduate than their counterparts at non-HBUs (Blake). Given the inequitable impact wrought by the pandemic on those students and, more recently, the elimination of affirmative action programs at elite public and private colleges, HBCCs and HBUs will play an even larger role as "ultimate emancipators."

Works Cited

"About Us." Shorter College. 2023. https://www.shortercollege.edu/about-us/.

Allen, Walter R., et al. "Historically Black Colleges and Universities: Honoring the Past, Engaging the Present, Touching the Future." *The Journal of Negro Education,* Summer 2007, vol. 76, no. 3, pp. 263–80.

Bailey, Thomas, et al. "Is Student-Right-to-Know All You Should Know of Community College Graduation Rates?" Community College Research Center. June 2005. https://ccrc.tc.columbia.edu/media/k2/attachments/analysis-community-college-grad-rates.pdf.

Blake, Jessica. "HBCUs Increase Black Students' Likelihood of Graduating." *Inside Higher Ed.* 29 Nov. 2023. https://www.insidehighered.com/news/quick-takes/2023/11/29/hbcus-increase-black-students-likelihood-graduating?utm_source=Inside+Higher+Ed&utm_campaign=9040868938-DNU_2021_COPY_02&utm_medium=email&utm_term=0_1fcbc04421-9040868938-198437221&mc_cid=9040868938&mc_eid=820b4005e4.

"The Brick School Legacy." Franklin Center at Brick. 23 April 2011. https://franklintoncenteratbricks.org/2011/04/23/the-brick-school-legacy/.

Early, Gerald. "The Quest for a Black Humanism." *Daedalus,* Spring 2006, vol. 135, no. 2, pp. 91–104.

Edmondson, Jasmine. "A Brief History: The Rise of Historically Black Colleges and Universities." 2023. https://www.lsu.edu/intlpro/apa/blog_posts/2021/hbcus_a_brief_history.php.

Elliott, Kayla C., et al. "Historically Black Community Colleges: A Descriptive Profile and Call for Context-Based Future Research." *Community College Journal of Research and Practice*, vol. 43, no. 10-11, 2019, pp. 770–84.

Fisher, Holly. "Oakwood College Students' Quest for Social Justice before and during the Civil Rights Era." *The Journal of African American History*, Spring 2003, vol. 88, no. 2, pp. 110–25.

Galizio, Lawrence, and George R. Boggs. "The Important History of Community Colleges." *Diverse Issues in Higher Education*, 28 Feb. 2022. https://www.diverseeducation.com/opinion/article/15288858/the-important-history-of-community-colleges.

Gassman, Marybeth. "The Unique Role of the HBCU Community College." 6 April 2015. https://hbculifestyle.com/the-unique-role-of-the-hbcu-community-college/.

Gilyard, Keith. "African American Contributions to Composition Studies." *College Composition and Communication*, vol. 50, no. 4, 1999, pp. 626–44.

Gold, David. *Rhetoric at the Margins: Revising the History of Writing Instruction in American Colleges, 1873–1947*. Southern Illinois UP, 2008.

"HBCUs Make America Strong: The Positive Economic Impact of Historically Black Colleges and Universities." United Negro College Fund. n.d. https://cdn.uncf.org/.

"Historical Sketch." St. Phillip's College. 2023. https://myspccatalog.alamo.edu/content.php?catoid=251&navoid=19420#St._Philip_s_College_Mission.

Jackson, Karen Keaton, et al. "We Belong in the Discussion: Including HBCUs in Conversations about Race and Writing." *College Composition and Communication*, vol. 71, no. 2, 2019, pp. 184–214.

Jarrett, Susan C. "Classics and Counterpublics in Nineteenth-Century Historically Black Colleges." *College English*, vol. 72, no. 2, 2009, pp. 134–59.

Lane, David. "The Junior College Movement among Negroes." *Journal of Negro Education*, vol. 3, no. 2, 1933, pp. 272–83.

Lovitt, Bobby L. *America's Historically Black Colleges and Universities: A Narrative History, 1837–2009*. Mercer UP, 2015.

"Mission." *St. Philip's College.* 2023. https://myspccatalog.alamo.edu/content.php?catoid=251&navoid=19420#St._Philip_s_College_Mission.

Morgan, Joan. "Little-Known, Little-Recognized: Historically Black Community Colleges Defy Categorization, Get Job Done." *Diverse Issues in Higher Education,* 16 June 2007, https://www.diverseeducation.com/students/article/15083627/little-known-little-recognized-historically-black-community-colleges-defy-categorization-get-job-done.

Moss, Beverly. "Where Would We Be? Legacies, Roll Calls, and the Teaching of Writing at HBCUs." *Composition Studies,* vol. 49, no. 1, 2021, pp. 144–48.

"On Their Own Terms: Two-Year Minority Serving Institutions." n.d. https://cmsi.gse.rutgers.edu/sites/default/files/MSI_CCreport_FINAL.pdf.

Royster, Jacqueline Jones, and Jean C. Williams. "History in the Spaces Left: African American Presence and Narratives of Composition Studies." *College Composition and Communication,* vol. 50, no. 4, 1999, pp. 563–84.

Seymour, Sean, and Julie Ray. "Grads of Historically Black Colleges Have Well-Being Edge." *Gallup.* 27 Oct. 2015. https://news.gallup.com/poll/186362/grads-historically-black-colleges-edge.aspx.

Strayhorn, Terrell. "Lessons Learned from Institutional Responses to COVID-19: Evidence-Based Insights from a Qualitative Study of Historically Black Community Colleges." *Community College Journal,* vol. 26, no. 1-2, 2021. https://doi.org/10.1080/10668926.2021.1975173.

Zaluda, Scott. "Lost Voices of the Harlem Renaissance: Writing Assigned at Howard, 1919–1931." *College Composition and Communication,* vol. 50, no. 2, 1998, pp. 232–57.

CHAPTER FIFTEEN

Decolonizing Assessment to Reveal Abundance: Crafting Threshold Concepts and Mapping Learning Journeys

JENNIFER TRAINOR
San Francisco State University

TARA LOCKHART
San Francisco State University

JOHN HOLLAND
San Francisco State University

ROBERT KOHLS
San Francisco State University

Writing program assessment often conjures a sense of lack, threatening to expose student—and teacher—deficits. As such, program assessment usually lands hardest on students of color, working-class students, multilingual and first-generation students, whose linguistic practices are hidden because they fail to meet the standards of White English still dominant in writing programs. Program assessment also alienates writing teachers, especially those of us who are part time and hence vulnerable to assessments that purport to reveal problems in our teaching. For these reasons, following Stephanie West-Puckett, Nicole I. Caswell, and William P. Banks, we argue that traditional assessment too often undermines progressive educational goals.

In this paper, we describe our attempt to decolonize program assessment, bringing it into alignment with our progressive goals. We replaced learning outcomes with threshold concepts in order to better capture teachers' learning goals in our classes. More important, we rejected rubrics because they are associated with criteria and mastery, and because they often promote an a-contextual vision of writing that, as Jennifer Randall's two 2021 articles suggest, ends up encoding white mainstream English.

Instead, we created a learning map that took an asset-based approach to student writing. Following Randall's four principles of antiracist assessment ("Color-neutral," 83), we eliminated language that echoed white supremacist literacy practices (e.g., "mastery"), included a consideration of the affective economies that circulate around literacy education, took care to locate students' struggles in their material/institutional conditions, and drew on teacher expertise at every turn.

Our efforts revealed abundance rather than deficit in students' literacy, and provided opportunities for lecturer-faculty collaboration, professional development, and leadership. Our approach to assessment revitalized our writing program by drawing on the participation and expertise of over 70% of our lecturer faculty (represented here by author John Holland) alongside three generations of WPAs (Trainor, Lockhart, and Kohls). Ultimately, our program assessment spurred lecturer-faculty leadership, scholarship, and curricular creativity, as well as an assessment model more attuned to our students' literacy strengths.

These changes were a significant pivot, since across our Cal State campus (urban, public, R2, HSI and AANAPISI), many stakeholders have a default belief in outcomes-based, rubric-driven, direct assessment of student "mastery"—the kind of assessment that satisfies accreditors but creates tensions for progressive writing programs like ours. Thus, when our campus required an assessment of our classes, we knew we had to take a different approach. Drawing on April Baker-Bell and Asao Inoue, we created a program assessment process that privileged lecturer-faculty expertise, used qualitative methods to unveil and interpret students' literacies and learning, and centered linguistic diversity as a primary value. Five years in, the result: rather than lack, we have uncovered—and created—abundance. Over the last five years, we have collected 2,000 pieces of student writing, mapped student learning trajectories rather than "mastery," and interpreted student writing in terms of what we value. This process has uncovered abundant student literacy practices and the "affective economies" (West-Puckett et al.) that attend them. It has helped us locate "failure" in institutional spaces and systems rather than students and teachers.

From Judging Writing to Interpreting Learning: Our Method

How did we reconcile institutional requirements for program assessment—including, on our campus, a requirement that we measure learning using a generic rubric—with the values and practices of "slow assessment" (Lindquist 2012)? How did we ensure that our assessment reflected linguistic justice and antiracist values? What did it mean, in our program, to decolonize assessment (see the Michigan State University Libraries guide), rescue it from the "improvement imperative" (Oleksiak 2022), and align it with progressive goals?

April Baker-Bell argues that rubrics are steeped in colonizing ideology that privileges White Mainstream English (WME) while silencing and further marginalizing the voices of students (2020). Rubrics claim to say something about what a program or teacher values, but the reality is that rubrics often represent an idealized, white mainstream version of "good writing"—a checklist of criteria—that is itself at odds with what teachers often actually care about.

Rubrics lead readers to judge rather than interpret student writing and learning. As important, rubrics too often focus our attention on end goals, warping the process of learning by obscuring the change and growth that happens in our classrooms. That growth is not typically captured by rubrics.

Thus, we sought to reimagine assessment and eschew judgment by valuing how students name what they know in a reflection-centered assignment, co-designed by teachers in our program. When reading these reflections for program assessment, we invited teachers to interpret student learning rather than judge student "mastery." And we conceptualized what students told us in their reflections as stops along our learning map, a map teachers created that included what West-Puckett, Caswell, and Banks call "sideways paths"—those detours and seemingly unrelated stops that students often take. The learning map consisted primarily of teachers' descriptions of typical students' progress rather than mastery of outcomes.

We began by asking teachers to bring in student writing that represented success in their classrooms, and used Broad's dynamic criteria mapping to ascertain our program's key values. We immediately noticed that teachers valued not performance but *learning*, and that meant that they often looked for metacognitive signals of growth or change in students' approach, affect, or literacy identity. They identified moments in student writing that indicated struggle toward new awareness, emerging confidence, engagement, and ownership of learning.

Once we recognized this mismatch between what teachers value in student writing and the traditional ways we have of measuring student "mastery," we set about creating new program assessment materials. We focused on *understandings* (Adler-Kassner and Wardle) rather than *judgments* about the so-called quality of students' so-called writing (Gallagher). Our choice in framing program assessment around threshold concepts came from a space of appreciation of slow learning that develops organically as students experience a course, and thus "slow assessment" (Lindquist 2012) focused on community sense-making with teachers. Our program assessment thus shifted the focus from learning objectives to how students come to understand themselves as writers as they experience a slowly unfolding course.

Through several iterations of these materials, we worked to describe students' journeys in ways that reflected our progressive goals. Instead of the deficit language of traditional rubrics ("thorough; adequate; minimal; appropriate; basic"), we reframed "failure" as "struggle toward" or "emergent" and located the sources of those struggles in students' lived and material experiences in educational institutions. Importantly, in order to avoid the white language supremacy that is often encoded in traditional assessment materials, we took a rhetorical and critical approach, creating a threshold concept focused on language and power, rather than grammatical correctness. Similarly, we built on, and revised for our context, the threshold concepts in Adler-Kassner and Wardle's *Naming What We Know*, embracing the metacognitive and affective dimensions of literacy in our learning map. Because our map is considerably more expansive than a traditional rubric (we have five descriptions of learning for each of our seven threshold concepts), it helps us capture what West Puckett, Caswell, and Banks call students' "sideways" learning journeys. Whereas rubrics list criteria, our learning map uses thick descriptions of students' emerging understanding.

To give you a sense of what our learning map looks like: our first threshold concept is *Writing requires engagement and agency; writers bring their voices, lived experiences, and identities to their work*. The learning map describes students as *emerging* at the beginning of the term and locates their struggles in institutional failures: students have not been authorized (by former schooling experiences) to use their voice, self, experience, or identity in their writing; students have been made to write without the use of "I" in their writing. Midway, many students begin to recognize that they can in fact use their voice in their academic writing. By the end of the semester, we hope students understand not only that they're allowed to bring their identity and voice to the page, but that doing so is important, a way to connect and engage with their audience and their learning. At the far end of our learning map, students can articulate meta-understandings of the threshold concept: Students can take an active role in using writing to connect their identities and voice with their audience and purpose. (To view the seven program-specific threshold concepts we developed, as well as the learning maps for each concept, readers can visit our Writing Program Assessment webpage.)

Assessment as Professional Development

In addition to uncovering abundance in student writing, our abundant assessment approach became a means of engaged professional development with faculty across ranks. Rooted in a community of practice (CoP) philosophy (Lave & Wenger, 1991; Wenger, 1998), our assessment project became a way for our faculty to explore what kinds of learning we aim for and how we support that learning through our teaching. Enacting *slow research* practices across several years, small groups of faculty met weekly for a semester to read student reflections and interpret student learning.

Teachers often report feeling alienated or threatened by traditional program assessment. In contrast, CoP participants in our program described a restorative and meaningful professional development and assessment experience. Specifically, participants noted axiological (what we value), ontological (how we understand reality), and epistemological (what and how we know) shifts that moved away from capitalist and white supremacist orientations (see Indigenous science scholar Megan Bang). As one of the participating teachers wrote after participating in our program assessment, "*Self-study meet-ups gave me permission to embrace, nurture, and guide messy student writing. . . . These meetings widened my tunnel vision regarding how the writing process may be messy before it finds clarity. My five colleagues said: look . . . there is meaning in the mess of student writing, there is meaning in bearing witness to your students discovering who they are and what they think through jumbled, even self-contradictory, writing.*"

By mapping learner trajectories vertically across our curriculum, including sideways paths as well as the material realities that impact students' paths, and by doing this work together in a CoP, our faculty deepened our abilities to describe the variations and complexities of students' development over time. It also allowed us to honor and affirm student learning journeys, especially when those journeys may have not matched our prior expectations. Acknowledging the range of student learning experiences in our classes in turn allowed us to collectively learn more deeply from those experiences, and to use student experiences as a lens back on our curricula and pedagogical practices. As Diab et al. advise, "collective interpretation of narratives—that is, testifying and processing together—is crucial to collective recognition of our problems, our commitments to counter them, and our efforts toward making commitments actionable" (6). Through program assessment that seeks to capture and understand the widest possible range of learning, we also not only center a more diverse and accurate understanding of our student population by "de-normalizing" whiteness and white supremacy culture (Jones and Okun, 2001), but we use the insights gleaned to "make room for nontraditional and/or disadvantaged minority students in the writing classroom" through faculty development aimed specifically at closing equity gaps and ensuring access (Sanchez and Branson, 50).

We conclude that using threshold concepts, instead of standardized rubrics or even student learning outcomes (SLOs), and replacing the toxicity of "mastery" with the metaphor of learning journeys, creates room for "new stories, new ways of collaborating, and new ways of living" (Diab et al. 2) that outcomes-based assessment does not. Tying authentic assessment to how we equitably enact programmatic goals and values is deeply contextual, meaningful, and necessarily collaborative work. CoP members who joined us in assessment work over the last five years found the work invigorating, and at times even transformational; they were more inspired to innovate and collaborate, and they felt more a part of our program and less isolated in their teaching. Our assessment approach strengthened our primarily contingent faculty's sense of community throughout and beyond the pandemic, and has helped us align our individual curricular approaches to our shared social and anti-racist pedagogical goals. Rather than an assessment approach that centered judgment and deficit (for both teacher and student), we created program assessment tools and practices that empowered faculty to see the diverse journeys our students take as they move through our courses.

Works Cited

Adler-Kassner, Linda, and Elizabeth Wardle. *Naming What We Know: Threshold Concepts of Writing Studies.* UP of Colorado, 2015.

Baker-Bell, April. *Linguistic Justice: Black Language, Literacy, Identity, and Pedagogy.* Routledge and NCTE, 2020.

Bang, Megan. "Learning on the Move Toward Just, Sustainable, and Culturally Thriving Futures." *Cognition and Instruction,* vol. 38, no. 3, 2020, pp. 434–44.

Bang, Megan, et al. "Undoing Human Supremacy and White Supremacy to Transform Relationships: An Interview with Megan Bang and Ananda Marin." *Curriculum Inquiry,* vol. 52, no. 2, 2022, pp. 150–61.

Broad, Bob. *What We Really Value: Beyond Rubrics in Teaching and Assessing Writing.* UP of Colorado, 2003.

Diab, Rasha, et al. "Making Commitments to Racial Justice Actionable." *Across the Disciplines: A Journal of Language, Learning and Academic Writing,* vol. 10, no. 3, 2013. DOI: https://doi.org/10.37514/ATD-J.2013.13.3.10

Gallagher, Chris W. "The Trouble with Outcomes: Pragmatic Inquiry and Educational Aims." *College English,* vol. 75, no. 1, 2012, pp. 42–60.

Jones, Kenneth, and Tema Okun. "White Supremacy Culture." *Dismantling Racism: A Workbook for Social Change Groups.* ChangeWork, 2001, pp. 28-35.

Lave, Jean, and Etienne Wenger. *Situated Learning: Legitimate Peripheral Participation.* Cambridge UP, 1991.

Lindquist, Julie. "Time to Grow Them: Practicing Slow Research in a Fast Field." *JAC,* vol. 32, no. 3-4, 2012, pp. 645–66.

Michigan State University Libraries Guide: Decolonize the University. libguides.lib.msu.edu/decolonize/classroom. Accessed 27 Feb. 2024.

Oleksiak, Timothy. "A Queer Praxis for Peer Review." *College Composition and Communication,* vol. 72, no. 2, 2020, pp. 306–22.

Randall, Jennifer, et al. "*Ain't* Oughta Be in the Dictionary: Getting to Justice by Dismantling Anti-Black Literacy Assessment Practices." *Journal of Adolescent & Adult Literacy,* vol. 64, no. 5, 2021, pp. 594–99.

Randall, Jennifer. "'Color-neutral' Is Not a Thing: Redefining Construct Definition and Representation through a Justice-Oriented Critical Antiracist Lens." *Educational Measurement: Issues and Practice,* vol. 40, no. 4, 2021, pp. 82–90.

Sanchez, James Chase, and Tyler S. Branson. "The Role of Composition Programs in De-Normalizing Whiteness in the University: Programmatic Approaches to Anti-Racist Pedagogies." *WPA: Writing Program Administration,* vol. 39, no. 2, 2016, pp. 47–52.

"SF State Writing Program Assessment Page." *Department of English Language and Literature,* SFSU, english.sfsu.edu/ge-writing/assessment. Accessed 17 July 2024.

Wenger, Etienne. *Communities of Practice: Learning, Meaning, and Identity.* Cambridge UP, 1999.

Decolonizing Assessment to Reveal Abundance

West-Puckett, Stephanie, et al. *Failing Sideways: Queer Possibilities for Writing Assessment.* UP of Colorado, 2023.

*This book was typeset in Sabon by Barbara Frazier.
The typeface used on the cover is DIN 2014 Rounded VF-Regular.
The book was printed on 50-lb. paper.*

www.ingramcontent.com/pod-product-compliance
Lightning Source LLC
Jackson TN
JSHW012048240625
86628JS00002B/2